LIVING IN THE RICHES OF HIS GRACE

CAS MONACO

LIVING IN THE RICHES OF HIS GRACE

A Devotional Bible Study
on the Book of Ephesians

Thru A Dirty Window
501 Finsbury St. #303
Durham, NC 27703

www.thruadirtywindow.wordpress.com
www.facebook.com/thruadirtywindow

All rights reserved.

No part of this work may be
reproduced or transmitted in any form
or by any means, electronic or mechanical,
including photocopying and recording, or by
any information storage or retrieval system,
except as may be expressly permitted by the
1976 Copyright Act or in writing from the
publisher. Requests for permission should
be addressed to Cas Monaco,
501 Finsbury St. #303 Durham, NC 27703

6th printing, June 2012

All Scripture
New American Standard Bible
Reference Edition,
LaHabra: A.J. Holman Company, 1960.

*To Charmaine, Anya, and Luda:
The Lord used each of you to shape me and my
walk with the Lord during our years in Russia.
You are truly kindred spirits.*

CONTENTS

Acknowledgments ❖ i

Introduction ❖ iii

A Word About the Word ❖ 1

The Riches of His Grace ❖ 15

The Richness of Relationship ❖ 35

The Riches of His Mercy ❖ 55

Brought Near by His Blood ❖ 79

His Amazing Love ❖ 99

Walk in a Manner Worthy ❖ 119

Walk in Newness of Life ❖ 141

Walk in Love ❖ 163

Walk in Obedience ❖ 185

Stand Firm in His Strength ❖ 205

Pray, Pray, Pray ❖ 229

Bibliography ❖ 251

Note Pages ❖ 252

ACKNOWLEDGMENTS

Thank you Janean, Sarita, Deb, Kristi, Karen, and Beth for all your faithful work on each lesson of this study. I appreciate more than you'll ever know your love for the Lord and knowledge of the Word. Without your help, I would have been lost. Thank you.

Thank you Jill for everything you do. I love you and am thankful every day for you.

LIVING IN THE RICHES OF HIS GRACE

It was springtime in Austin, Texas, and the year was 1991. I was alone in my home packing boxes, getting ready to move. My husband, Bob, and I had been on the staff of Campus Crusade for Christ for a number of years, several of which had been at the University of Texas in Austin. I was packing up our things because the Lord had called us to a one-year short-term mission to serve in the then Soviet Union. Historically the opportunity for ministry was unprecedented. Not many years before, the foreboding wall separating Western Europe from Eastern Europe, and separating freedom from communism, had fallen. Communism was crumbling along with all of its ideologies, providing new opportunities for the Gospel to go forward.

Bob and I made a commitment to spend a year in the city of Moscow, leading a team of six men and women. Our job was to take the Gospel of Jesus Christ to students on the campus of Moscow State University. While I was excited by the prospect, I was also frightened and apprehensive at the thought of living in another country—especially Russia! As I carefully wrapped each of my favorite teacups and porcelain treasures, I remember saying out loud, "Lord, I look forward to unpacking all of my treasures this time next year." Yet, I had this foreboding feeling I would still be in the Soviet Union a year later, an idea, which did not appeal to me very much!

In late September 1991 we arrived in Moscow with about 50 other Campus Crusade for Christ staff and students. Most of the others would be traveling to other cities within the Soviet Union, while two teams remained in Moscow—ours being one of them. We arrived just weeks after a military coup, and the kidnapping of Mikhail Gorbechov. There was a sense of tremendous unrest, and just three months later communism dissolved. The Soviet flag was lowered in Red Square and the Russian flag was raised. Not only was there vast political and economic change, but also a fantastic change was taking place in the hearts of the people.

For 70 years Lenin had been revered and worshipped. In every meeting room and on nearly every major corner there was a statue in Lenin's likeness, and in every textbook Lenin and his ideologies were the central subject. One young student told us when communism fell and he realized Lenin's teachings were not true, a huge emptiness entered his soul. And there we were to fill that emptiness with the truth of Jesus Christ.

Bob and I lived in Moscow for nearly three years. They were three of the most intense, challenging, and incredible years of my life. Words cannot express the privilege it was to serve in a country where hearts were so open to the truth of Jesus Christ. They were also three of the most spiritually deepening years of my life. Many of us on our team laughed at the thought that the Lord had to take us halfway around the world and place us into a completely foreign environment to finally get our attention. We had come to share the life-changing gospel of Jesus Christ and, in the process, our lives were being forever changed.

Dig deep into the storehouses of His Word to find the rich truths He has provided for all of us who believe.

It was during my years in Moscow that I began to study the book of Ephesians. Perhaps it was because everything familiar was stripped away and a new kind of dependence on the Lord was required that I found the rich truths of Ephesians to be nourishing and satisfying. I spent many a morning in my little Russian kitchen, being warmed by my stove and ministered to by the Word, marveling at the relationship God initiated with me. The truth of the Gospel of Jesus Christ, His work on the cross, His rich grace and mercy and His choice of me is so clearly and wonderfully described in Ephesians. It caused me to worship Him and to thrill at the thought of telling others how they could have a relationship with the only true God! Throughout our study, I will share with you ways the Lord used His Word in my own life as I faced life and ministry in another country. I will also encourage you to dig deep into the storehouses of His Word to find the rich truths He has provided for all of us who believe.

As you begin your study of Ephesians, let me explain to you how I have designed this study. Each lesson in this study guide is broken down into five sections. Each day you will find a reminder to read through Ephesians once. While you work through the lesson each day, I will encourage you to look at related passages throughout the Bible and you will have the opportunity to apply the Word to your own life. The fifth section of each lesson is reserved for reflection, prayer, and worship as you wrap up the passage of the week. Let me encourage you to take your time and enjoy the truths of God's Word.

I am hoping and praying your study of the book of Ephesians will encourage and motivate you as it has me. I pray you will find your heart and your mind centered on the Savior in fresh ways as you study this treasure chest of truth. As you begin your study, pray through the prayer of Ephesians 1:17-19. Pray that "the eyes of your heart may be enlightened so that you may know what is the hope of His calling, what are the riches of the glory of His inheritance in the saints, and what is the surpassing greatness of His power toward you as a believer."

"I pray that the eyes of your heart may be enlightened, so that you may know what is the hope of His calling, what are the riches of the glory of His inheritance in the saints, and what is the surpassing greatness of His power toward us who believe."

Ephesians 1:18-19

LESSON 1

A Word about the Word

DAY ONE

☐ Read Ephesians

As a young believer, I was influenced by a little book Robert Shirock wrote entitled, "Studying God's Word and Loving It." He encouraged his readers to choose a reliable translation and to purchase a good, sturdy Bible that is enjoyable to pick up and read and that will be around for a long time. My Bible-reading friends encouraged me to choose a readable format I could stay with for my lifetime. They explained to me that I would become more and more familiar with my Bible and would easily be able to recall certain verses or passages because I could "picture" the page in my mind. They were right!

In this study I will use the New American Standard Bible, but there are other reliable translations. Let me encourage you to find a Bible you're comfortable with and one you will look forward to picking up and reading. Collect a few extras that are the same format, just in case your first one wears out! I can guarantee you you will reap the same rewards I have.

DAY TWO

☐ Read Ephesians

Ephesians was written between the years 60 and 62 AD. Its human author was the apostle Paul and its words were divinely inspired by the Holy Spirit of God. As we begin today's lesson we are going to look at the life of Paul, as well as the spiritual climate of the city of Ephesus. As you begin your time in the Word today, pray the words of Psalm 119:18: "Open my eyes that I may behold wonderful things from Thy law."

We will begin our look into Paul's life in the book of Acts. The book of Acts is the history of the early Christian church. Acts begins with the ascension of Christ immediately following His great commandment to "go into all the world and preach the Gospel to all the nations." The early chapters of Acts record great numbers of people coming to faith in Jesus Christ, but not without great persecution. In Acts, we are introduced to Paul before he ever knew Jesus Christ as his Lord and Savior. In order to set the stage, we first need to meet Stephen.

1. In Acts 6, we are introduced to a man named Stephen who had just been appointed as a deacon in the early church. Read Acts 6:2-8 and record what you learn about Stephen.

2. According to Acts 6:9-15, of what was Stephen accused? To whom was he "dragged off" to see?

3. Stephen briefly recounts much of the Old Testament to his Jewish accusers, pointing out God's continual deliverance and faithfulness in the face of Israel's disobedience and rebellion. Like their forefathers, the Jews of his day rejected the truth of Jesus Christ. Of what does Stephen accuse his accusers in Acts 7:51-53?

4. What was the reaction to Stephen according to Acts 7:54-60?

5. What do you observe about Stephen as he faces death?

6. Read Acts 7:58-8:3. To whom are we introduced? What kind of man was he? Use Scripture to support your answer.

7. Look at Acts 9:1-2. Some time has passed since the death of Stephen, and Saul was continuing to "ravage" the church (body of believers). How do these verses describe Saul? What was his plan?

8. Read Paul's statements about himself in Acts 22:2-5 and Philippians 3:4-6. Based upon what you have learned, what motivated Saul (who was later called "Paul")? In other words, was he merely a murderous criminal or did something greater motivate him and, if so, what? Use Scripture to support your answer.

9. Now that you have been introduced to both Stephen and Saul, what do you observe they had in common? What was it that compelled them?

10. What differences between the two men do you observe, and what was the reason for their differences?

Reflection

As you finish your study, take some time to thank the Lord for the great purpose He gives us for living. Thank Him for men like Stephen who stood firm in the midst of persecution, and yet remained Christ-centered. Thank Him for the example Stephen is for us today. Pray that believers everywhere would be bold in their witness for Christ, choosing to live every day for Christ.

DAY THREE

☐ Read Ephesians

Saul, a Hebrew of Hebrews and a member of the Sanhedrin (the ruling Jewish council of his day), was a great persecutor of the early church. He was present at the stoning death of Stephen and was, in fact, in hearty agreement with his murder. Saul was doing what he believed was right in protecting himself and the Jews of his day from Jesus Christ.

1. Read Acts 9:1-2. For what purpose was Saul going to Damascus? Look closely at the text.

2. According to Acts 9:3-4, what happened to Saul on the road to Damascus? With what question was Saul presented?

3. Who had Saul been persecuting? Why is it significant that the Lord asked, "Why are you persecuting Me?"

4. According to Acts 9:5, what was Saul's response?

5. What did the Lord Jesus tell Saul to do and how did Saul respond? What did his traveling companions do? Look carefully at Acts 9:6-9 for your answers.

6. Read Acts 9:10-16. The Lord appeared to Ananias in a vision and told him about Saul's conversion. What is his response when the Lord told him to go and find Saul?

7. What do you learn about the Lord's purpose for Saul in these verses?

8. For what reason was Ananias to go and find Saul? According to Acts 9:17-22, what happened when Ananias laid hands on Saul? Look closely for several answers.

9. Read Acts 9:23-25. How did the Jews respond to Saul's conversion?

10. In Acts 9:26-30 what do you find Saul doing? How did the believers respond to his conversion?

11. What do you learn about the grace and mercy of God from Saul's conversion? What do you learn about the Lord's grace and mercy in your own life?

12. Look carefully at II Corinthians 5:17. How do you see this truth to be true in Saul's life? How do you see this truth to be true in your own life?

Reflection

Take some time to thank the Lord for saving you! Thank Him for transforming your life, for making you a new creature in Christ. Thank Him for the picture of His grace and mercy in Saul's life and in your life!

DAY FOUR

☐ Read Ephesians

In Acts 13, following his dramatic conversion, Saul's name is changed to Paul and we learn of his unique call to take the Gospel of Jesus Christ to the Gentiles. It is also in this chapter that we begin to follow Paul on his many missionary journeys. Because he wrote most of the New Testament epistles, it is easy to see Paul's passionate love for Christ. We often read about his commitment to believers and his desire for all men everywhere to be saved—both Jew and Gentile alike.

Before you begin your study, pray the Lord will give you wisdom and insight as you spend time with Him.

1. For review and instruction, read Acts 22:1-21. Paul takes the opportunity to share his testimony with the people in Jerusalem. Read these verses carefully and make note of the way he shares the Gospel using his own conversion as an example.

    a. How does Paul describe himself before he knew Christ?

    b. How does he describe his encounter with Christ?

    c. What changes took place in his life?

d. For what reason was he in Jerusalem?

2. TRUTH SEARCH

   Read the following passages and record your observations about Paul and his love for the Lord. Consider the difference Jesus Christ made in his life, his purpose and his goals. Romans 1:14-17; I Corinthians 2:1-5; 15:1-11; Ephesians 3:8; 4:1; 6:19-20; Philippians 3:3-14.

3. Read Acts 19:1-7. Upon arriving in Ephesus, what did Paul discover? How did he respond?

4. According to Acts 19:8-20, what were the extraordinary miracles Paul performed? How would you describe the response to the Gospel?

5. In Acts 19:23-34 we read about a rather large disturbance in Ephesus. What started this disturbance? What words are used to describe this disturbance?

6. Read Acts 19:35-20:1. How was the rioting stopped?

7. What have you learned about Ephesus from this chapter in Acts?

8. As you consider the spiritual climate surrounding you, in what ways is your city like Ephesus?

Reflection

Having a good understanding of doctrine, or the essential truths of Christianity, is crucial when it comes to facing unbelief in our neighborhoods, schools, and workplaces. Pray the Lord will help you grasp and understand His Word so you can stand firm for Him.

Thank the Lord for saving you. Whether you were born again as a small child or have just recently trusted Jesus Christ as your Savior and Lord, never stop praising Him for saving you! Ask Him to empower you to be His witness.

DAY FIVE

The fifth day of every lesson has been set aside for meditation and reflection. I want to encourage you to *not* pass by this day, but to enjoy spending time thinking about and thanking the Lord for what you are learning. Take this day to go back over the previous four, recall what you have learned and ask yourself, "What is God teaching me?"

1. Take time to read Ephesians aloud. I like to read aloud because sometimes I hear things I would miss otherwise. Enjoy the truths of Ephesians and continue to pray He will teach you more and more about Him as you spend time in His Word.

2. Thank the Lord for the transforming power of the Gospel. Thank Him for saving you. Thank Him for rescuing you, as He did Paul, from the penalty of sin. Thank Him for using you, as He did Paul, to take the Gospel to unbelievers. Thank Him that you are "His workmanship, created in Christ Jesus for good works, which God prepared beforehand that we should walk in them." (Ephesians 2:10)

3. Are there people in your life with whom you need to share your testimony—maybe a co-worker, a family member, the person who cuts your hair, or your dentist? Pray that the Lord will give you boldness and courage to talk about how Jesus Christ has changed your life.

Optional Exercise

How well are you able to "proclaim the excellencies of Christ?" If you've never written down how you came to know Christ as your Lord and Savior, follow the guidelines below:

1. What were your attitudes, interests, and thoughts about God before you came to know Him personally?

2. How did God begin to work in your heart and life? (Consider how your attitudes were changing, whom He began using to tell you about Christ, etc.)

3. When and how did you place your faith in Christ?

4. What changes took place after you trusted Christ as your Savior?

5. Stop and thank Him right now for all He has done for you. Pray for an opportunity to tell someone this week about the changes Christ has made in your life.

"Blessed be the God and Father of our Lord Jesus Christ, who has blessed us with every spiritual blessing in the heavenly places in Christ, just as He chose us in Him before the foundation of the world, that we should be holy and blameless before Him."

Ephesians 1:3-4

LESSON TWO

The Riches of His Grace
Ephesians 1:1-14

Assigned to live in Moscow, a large looming city of over 14 million people, my husband and I and our six teammates moved into our flats (apartments) in the fall of 1991. A group of summer missionaries had set up a food delivery for us and the members of our team in an effort to save us time and energy. We were very grateful because shopping for necessities (like food and drink) could be, and was, quite a challenge.

The food delivery started out well. Once every two weeks we would receive a delivery of potatoes, apples, tomatoes (until the late fall), carrots and meat in quantities big enough for eight people. Our team would gather together and divide up our spoils. The amount of food was adequate—no more—no less than adequate. But towards the end of October, the deliveries were less and less dependable, and consequently we had less and less food. Before the winter set in we had been able to buy potatoes, onions, and tomatoes from the street vendors, but the snow and the cold temperatures brought an end to our "street shopping."

We weren't starving by any means, but we weren't being supplied with much either. All of us had brought plenty of provision from America, and there were a few "Western" stores in the city where we could stock up when we needed to. But there were a few nights throughout those late Fall months that Bob would lie in bed next to me and tell me, "I am so hungry!" The guys on our team all lost a lot of weight, too! We attempted to buy things in the state-run shops, but usually only cabbage and a few meager potatoes and onions were available. We not only felt bad for ourselves, but also for the Russians!

Tragically, many of us are living like spiritual paupers. The rich treasury of God's Word is right at our fingertips, but is often ignored or set aside.

In January, some friends from another city came to stay with us for a few days. Having spent a summer in Moscow, they were familiar with the city and were certain that in our area there was a farmer's market where they had stocked up on oranges and cashews. I laughed to myself thinking, "Oranges and cashews! They've got to be kidding! We can barely find the basics, let alone luxuries like oranges and cashews!" We decided to humor them and ventured out one morning in search of this so-called market.

That particular day (one which I doubt I will ever forget) was absolutely freezing! Yet unlike most winter days in Moscow, the sky was brilliantly bright and sunny, and a crystal clear blue. We made our way to the market by trolley bus, getting off just two stops from our flat. We waded through a huge group of street vendors—mostly older women—standing in the sub-zero weather selling everything from handmade mittens and household items to vodka and cigarettes. What a sight! What still amazes me today was those women stood holding their wares for the buyer to see, without mittens or gloves, in skirts in the freezing cold! Russians are so tenacious!

We approached a fenced area where the crowd grew thick and there was increased activity. As we walked through the gate past a little lady and her box of medicinal herbs, I can still remember the strong smell of pickles and pickled garlic cloves. We made our way toward a large square building, walked up the worn cement steps, opened the doors, and stepped into a huge open room. The sun was streaming in from the skylights above, shining gloriously on stacks and stacks of perfectly placed towers of oranges, apples, bananas and pineapples! Bob and I stopped dead in our tracks. Our mouths dropped open. "Food, glorious food!" We turned to look in another direction and found the dairy section. We walked past clean eggs (the best we'd seen in months were quail eggs), fresh creamy butter, milk, cream, and several different kinds of cheese. Just ahead was the meat section. The pork section was beneath the pig's head, the beef beneath the cow's head, and the chickens lay all in a row. There were potatoes, cucumbers, lettuce, onions, and a section reserved solely for several different kinds of homespun honey. A long row of beautiful long stemmed roses in a myriad of colors seemed to top everything off! We had been living like paupers when just within our reach were delicious "riches" for the buying!

As we continue our study of the book of Ephesians, I cannot help but remember our discoveries that day. As believers in Jesus Christ we have daily, minute-by-minute access to a rich and eternal treasury, one that has been provided for us by our loving Savior and Lord. Tragically, many of us are living like spiritual paupers. The rich treasury of God's Word is right at our fingertips, but is often ignored or set aside. We wonder why we are starving spiritually! It is my prayer that, as you open the pages of the Word of God and drink in His rich truth, you will stand in awe—just like Bob and I did when we walked into that building filled with food. I pray that you will return to His Word daily, eager to be filled with Him and His Word. Ephesians 1:1-14 is rich and sweet—just like the juicy orange I ate that day in Moscow! Dig in and enjoy!

DAY ONE

☐ Read Ephesians

Ephesus was a city located in the area we know today as Turkey. Ephesians was written primarily to the church in Ephesus (which was pastored by Paul's disciple, Timothy), but was also circulated throughout the surrounding region.

The theme of Ephesians is best summed up in Ephesians 1:3, "Blessed be the God and Father of our Lord Jesus Christ, who has blessed us with every spiritual blessing in the heavenly places in Christ Jesus." The first three chapters explain clearly what those spiritual blessings are—what our position is in Christ. Our position in Christ is absolutely sure in spite of our behavior because our position rests on the finished work of Christ on the cross. The last three chapters give us instruction on how to practically live, day to day, in light of our position.

Take some time to pray. Ask the Lord to give you wisdom as you read His Word. Pray that your heart will be prepared for the truth of His Word. Thank Him for giving you His Word!

1. Read through the first three chapters of Ephesians and record what you learn about God the Father.

2. What do you learn about God the Son?

3. What do you learn about God the Holy Spirit?

4. What do you observe about the apostle Paul in these three chapters?

5. Look specifically at Ephesians 1:3-4, 7, 9, 11, 13; 2:4-10 and 3:6. What things are true for the believer/child of God?

Reflection

Take some time to thank the Lord for His Word. Thank Him for the things you discovered as you read through Ephesians. Thank Him for His Son and thank Him that you stand complete in Christ. Thank Him for instruction on how to walk in a manner worthy of your calling. Thank Him for every spiritual blessing that is yours in Christ.

DAY TWO

☐ Read Ephesians

Ephesians 1:1-6

1. Read Ephesians 1:1-2. What do you learn about Paul? What do you learn about the believers in Ephesus?

2. Ephesians 1:3-14 is broken down into three sections, each section describing the role of the triune God in salvation. Look closely and see if you can determine where each section begins and ends. Use Scripture to support your answer. Look for the Father, the Son, and the Holy Spirit.

3. Today we are going to focus on God the Father, and His role in our salvation from eternity past. Read Ephesians 1:3-6 carefully and record everything the Father has done for us.

4. In whom did He bless, choose, and predestine us?

5. When did the Father choose us? For what purpose did the Father choose us in Christ? For additional insight see: Ephesians 1:6a.

6. Read Ephesians 1:3-6 again. What do you learn about the character of the Father in these verses? Keep your eyes on the text!

7. According to Romans 2:4 and Titus 3:4-7, what more do you learn about His kindness?

Reflection

As a new believer I remember learning that God chose me, He drew me to Himself and saved me from the penalty of my sin. I remember being told that, left to my own devices, I would have never chosen Him. I remember feeling angry and prideful, not wanting to admit that I had nothing to do with my salvation. But as I continued to study the Word of God and as I grew in my understanding of the depth of my sin, I found myself awestruck by the love of the Father. I began to marvel that He would send His only begotten Son to die in my place, and pay the penalty for sin that I committed against Him! Yes, there was a point when I stopped and placed my faith in Christ, but I soon learned that apart from Him drawing me to Himself I would not have made that decision. As one preacher put it: "I did the sinning, He did the saving!"

Take some time and thank the Lord for blessing you with "every spiritual blessing in the heavenly places in Christ."

Thank Him for choosing you to be holy and blameless before Him and for His love that predestined you to adoption. Thank Him that you are His child, and that He is your perfect, heavenly Father.

Thank Him for the "kind intention of His will," and for His kindness that leads to repentance.

Pray that you will live in such a way that will result in praise and glory and honor to Him.

DAY THREE

☐ Read Ephesians

Ephesians 1:6-14

1. Read through Ephesians 1-3 and, as you read, record every verse that mentions God's grace.

2. The Biblical definition for God's grace is an undeserved favor or an unmerited gift. Based upon your observations, in what way has God demonstrated His grace in the believer's life? Use Scripture to support your answer.

3. In Ephesians 1:3-6 we looked at the Father's eternal purpose for us in the past. Look closely at Ephesians 1:6-8. As you read, you will find Jesus Christ's eternal purpose for us in the present. What words are used to describe God's display of grace?

4. a. Define:
   Freely:

   Rich:

   Lavish:

   b. Why do you think Paul uses these words to describe grace?

5. What act of God describes His rich and lavish grace according to Ephesians 1:6-8?

6. TRUTH SEARCH

   The New Testament was originally written in the Greek language. We can often enhance our understanding of a word or passage by looking up the same word in the Greek dictionary. In Greek, redemption means: to release from captivity, to pay a ransom in order to release a person from bondage, especially that of slavery.

   a. Look up the following passages and record what you discover man's bondage to be: John 8:34; Romans 6:16; II Peter 2:19.

b. What is the result of slavery to sin? Ezekiel 18:4; Romans 3:23; 6:16-23; Ephesians 2:1, 5.

c. Why do you think we must grasp our bondage before we can fully appreciate God's grace?

7. According to the following passage, what two things were accomplished through the shed blood of Jesus Christ?

"It is through Him, at the cost of His own blood, that we are redeemed, freely forgiven through that full and generous grace which has overflowed into our lives and opened our eyes to the truth. For God has allowed us to know the secret of His plan, and it is this: He purposes in His sovereign will that all human history shall be consummated in Christ, that everything that exists in Heaven or earth shall find its perfection and fulfillment in Him." Ephesians 1:7-11[1]

8. What is the "secret of God's plan?" See Philippians 2:9-11 and Colossians 1:16-20 for additional insight.

9. According to Ephesians 1:11-12 what is the reason for our inheritance? We know our eternal future is secure in Christ. How can this make a difference in our day-to-day life?

10. Read Ephesians 1:13-14. For what ultimate purpose have we been predestined to adoption, given an inheritance, and sealed in Him with the Holy Spirit of promise? Use Scripture to support your answer.

Reflection

Once again, stop and marvel. Praise the Lord for redeeming you from slavery to sin and eternal separation from Him. Praise Him for His Beloved Son!

Read Ephesians 1:3-14 aloud. Insert your name in place of the word "us." As you walk through this passage, let the words sink into your heart. Thank Him for the rich truths found in these eleven verses. Pray and ask Him to help you understand and grasp these truths.

If you have read through these passages and have realized you are a slave to sin and you have never asked Christ to forgive you, do so right now. Confess your sin to God. Thank Him for choosing you before the foundation of the world, for redeeming you from the penalty of sin, and for lavishing His grace upon you.

DAY FOUR

☐ Read Ephesians

Ephesians 1:6-8

1. Review Ephesians 1:3-14, giving special attention to verses 6-7. Record the result of Christ's redeeming love.

2. There is nothing more freeing than understanding what it means to be redeemed, to be "set free" from slavery to sin as well as the penalty of sin. Forgiveness, as we learned in this passage in Ephesians, is undeserved (it's the result of God's grace). It is free and complete. Read the following verses and record what you learn about God's forgiveness: Colossians 2:13-14; I John 2:12.

3. In what ways does the Lord's forgiveness in your life help or encourage you day by day?

All of the things listed in Ephesians 1:3-14 are true for us as believers, regardless of our daily experience. They are true because of Jesus Christ, not because of us. He must be the centerpiece of our lives.

We must look to Him for assurance of salvation, the promise of forgiveness, and the hope of eternal life with Him. As we move along in our study of Ephesians, we will look more closely at how to walk with the Lord on a day-to-day basis. Until then, let me share something that has helped me put into practice the forgiveness that is mine in Him. This is something I learned after getting involved with Campus Crusade for Christ as a college student.

4. Colossians 2:13-14 says: "And when you were dead in your transgressions and the uncircumcision of your flesh, He made you alive together with Him, having forgiven us all our transgressions, having canceled out the certificate of debt consisting of decrees against us and which was hostile to us; and He has taken it out of the way, having nailed it to the cross."

    "In the day when this was written, 'list of sins' meant an itemized bond nailed to the prison cell door. It listed every crime for which the prisoner had been convicted. When the sentence was served or restitution paid, the authorities removed the list and wrote, "paid in full." The prisoner used this as proof that he could never be tried for those crimes again. The believer who trusts Christ's payment for sin can never be tried again. You have a full pardon from God."[2]

    a. What has God done with your sin? Use Scripture to support your answer.

    b. How many of your sins did Christ die for?

5. You can experience God's love and forgiveness every day. Even though you are totally forgiven, you still need to deal with your sins on a day-to-day basis in order to experience continuing fellowship with God. Let's look at how to restore your fellowship with God.

    a. Read I John 1:9. To confess means to agree with God about your sin, to thank Him for forgiving you at the cross, and to ask Him to change your actions and attitudes. By turning back to God and away from your sin, you will experience His love and forgiveness provided by Christ's death on the cross. Instead of experiencing guilt, condemnation and punishment, your fellowship with God will be restored.

Here is a simple way to put I John into practice:

1. Memorize I John 1:9.

2. Call it sin: Agree with God that you have sinned.

3. Call it forgiven: Agree that God has already forgiven you.

4. Call on God to change you: Trust God to change your attitudes and actions.

b. Based upon what you have studied so far, how often do you need to confess your sin to God?

6. Faith, or taking God at His Word, is the basis for experiencing God's forgiveness on a daily, moment-to-moment basis. Faith means taking God at His Word regardless of your feelings or circumstances.

a. What should you do if you still feel guilty after you have confessed your sin? Read Psalm 32:5; 103:12; Isaiah 43:25 for insight.

b. Will applying these truths affect your life?

Reflection

There is nothing more freeing than knowing you are completely forgiven. Thank the Lord for His forgiveness and for choosing you to be His child. Thank Him for sending His Son, and for initiating a relationship with you.

Look again at Ephesians 1:3-14 and record everything that is true for every person who is IN CHRIST. Then worship the Lord for all He has done for you.

DAY FIVE

☐ Read Ephesians

The past four days we have looked at some amazing truths! It is essential that, as believers, we never grow tired of worshipping the Lord for the gift of His Son and for the wonder of His grace. In eleven verses we have learned so much about what it means to be a child of God. We have looked closely at our position in Christ, a position that is absolutely secure. Thank the Lord often for choosing you, redeeming you, and for giving you the Holy Spirit as a down payment on your future inheritance.

Not only have we learned about what is true of us in Christ, but we have also learned something about the triune God. We have learned that God is our Father, that Jesus Christ is our Redeemer, and that the Holy Spirit is the pledge of our inheritance.

Take some time today and worship God. Pray that the Lord will teach you more about Him as you look into His Word.

1. Understanding that God is our heavenly Father is essential if we are to love Him and to be assured of His love. Spend time with your Father in His Word, which is His love letter to you. Look up the following verses and record what you learn about the Father.

    John 1:12

    John 10:28-29

    I John 1:1-3

    Galatians 4:4-7; Romans 8:15-16; 32-33.

2. What aspect of the fatherhood of God encourages you the most and why?

3. Remember that redemption means to be set free from bondage. Jesus Christ is your Redeemer—He has set you free! Meditate on the following verses with regard to your redemption and your Redeemer. Read and then write out the verses that are especially meaningful to you right now: Isaiah 43:25, 45:22; Micah 7:18; John 8:31-36; I John 1:7-9.

4. Jesus promised His disciples they would not be left alone. He said the Father would send them a Helper, the Holy Spirit. Read the following and record what you discover about the Holy Spirit: John 14:16-17,26; John 16:13; Romans 8:26-27; II Corinthians 3:6-8, 17.

5. In what ways has the Holy Spirit helped you, given you guidance, or reminded you of your freedom in Christ?

6. What have you learned this week that you didn't know before? What have you been reminded of that you have known for a long time?

Reflection

Take some time and praise the Lord for who He is. Ask Him to make you mindful of His presence, His attributes, and His purposes in your life. Pray that your life will be a reflection to those around you of His grace and love.

Copy Ephesians 1:1-14 in the back of your book. Copying Scripture is a great way to meditate on God's Word!

---

1 Phillips Translation, Eph. 1:7-11.
2 Campus Crusade, pg. 2.

"For this reason I too, having heard of the faith in the Lord Jesus which exists among you, and your love for all the saints, do not cease giving thanks for you, while making mention of you in my prayers; that the God of our Lord Jesus Christ, the Father of glory, may give to you a spirit of wisdom and of revelation in the knowledge of Him."

Ephesians 1:15-17

LESSON THREE

The Richness of Relationship
Ephesians 1:15-23

Moscow State University was our primary place of ministry, and reaching college students with the Gospel of Jesus Christ was our primary goal. Yet, in addition to sharing the Gospel and developing disciples on campus, we also desired to plant a church where the students we met could join us in worship. My husband, along with our pastor in Austin, Texas, had numerous talks about what that would look like and how to begin.

Our first Sunday service was held in our teammate's apartment. We stacked stools on top of each other for a pulpit, and arranged a couch and a couple of chairs in "church-like" formation. John, one of our team members, played his guitar and Bob preached from the book of I Thessalonians. There were only the eight of us that first week, but we enjoyed singing and worshipping together in our new surroundings.

Within about two weeks Bob and I were settled into our flat. It had two rooms and a kitchen. The living room was quite large and very adequate for church services during the first two months. Our congregation of eight was soon joined by the other team of Americans working with Campus Crusade for Christ in another part of the city. Word quickly spread to some other Americans living in the city, and in a very short time we had several students join us as well. Two months later we had nearly forty people attending! As the congregation grew, so did our needs. It was clear our flat was not going to be big enough for long, and we were in need of a translator because the students who attended were inviting their Russian-speaking friends and family.

> *We held our first services in the "Blue Theater," located just off the corner of Red Square and within a stone's throw of Lenin's Tomb!*

Kevin, a good friend of ours, shared Bob's vision for planting a church. He was eager and worked hard with Bob to find a suitable place for us to meet. Just after the first of the year (1992) we held our first services in the "Blue Theater," located just off the corner of Red Square and within a stone's throw of Lenin's Tomb! We added more musicians, someone to make announcements, a translator and a Sunday School for the children. Within a very short time there were not only students, but also their parents, grandparents, siblings, and friends. What an exciting time!

Knowing that he was not called to Russia to be a pastor, Bob began talking with an American pastor named Ronnie Stevens. After a series of conversations and sensing the call of God, Ronnie and his family moved to Moscow in the Fall of 1992. For the next three years Ronnie pastored Moscow Bible Church (MBC), and the Lord blessed the growth of our little church. As time went on, various Sunday School classes, prayer meetings, Bible studies and baptisms became a regular part of church life.

Oleg Shevkin, a former student at Moscow State University who had been involved with us early on and was often Ronnie's translator, traveled to Dallas Theological Seminary in the spring of 1993 to get his master's degree in theology. Oleg's plan was to return to Moscow and pastor this church! In the Spring of 1997, Oleg was installed as the first Russian pastor of MBC! In its first nine years the church has grown from eight to over 200 people. Several of the students involved with us in the beginning are now married, have children, and help with the ministry of the church.

Ephesians contains much information regarding the church—the body of believers. The prayer found in Ephesians 1:15-23 so clearly expresses the Lord's heart for His children, and for His church—that we would know Him and understand what He has done for us in His Son. When I think back over the years of prayer and hard work that have gone into Moscow Bible Church, I am humbled to think of the Lord's faithfulness in building a strong body of believers through the ministry of Moscow Bible Church. Not only have many been saved through the ministry of that body of believers, but also many have continued to grow and bear fruit in His name and for His glory. When I think of and pray for MBC, I can identify with Paul as He remembered the love and faith of the believers in Ephesus. I join with him in praying for the continuing growth of the church in Russia.

As you begin your study today, join with me in praying through the prayer of Ephesians 1:15-23 for Moscow Bible Church and your own life!

DAY ONE

☐ Read Ephesians

Ephesians 1:15-17

1. Read Ephesians 1:15-16. For what two reasons was Paul thankful?

    a. According to John 13:34 and I John 3:14-16, what is the distinguishing mark of a child of God? Why?

    b. What does this tell you about the Ephesian church?

2. Read Ephesians 1:15-17. What is the main thing that Paul asks of "the God of our Lord Jesus Christ, the Father of glory?"

3. Why is this request significant?

Did you notice as you read this passage that Paul prays for believers to know Christ? He does not give us instructions on how to live, but instead prays we would grow in our understanding of Him! It is so encouraging to realize the God of the universe desires for us to really know Him! Not only does He desire that we grow in wisdom and understanding, but He also provides us with His Word. Without spending regular time in the Word of God, even the most eager and sincere believer will not be able to grow in wisdom and understanding.

4. As you have considered Ephesians 1:3-14, and all that God has done for us in Christ, what do you know about Him so far?

5. TRUTH SEARCH

   a. As you look up the following verses, record some things the Lord wants you to know about Him: Job 19:25; Jeremiah 9:23-24; John 10:14,15, 27-30.

   b. According to these passages, how would you describe a heart that desires to know the Lord? Psalm 27:4-6; Psalm 73:25-28; Philippians 3:7-11. How would you describe your heart toward the Lord?

c. Look up Psalm 9:10, Psalm 46:1-3, and II Peter 1:2-3, and record some of the results of knowing Him. Ask yourself, "Am I experiencing these results in my relationship with Him?"

Reflection

Take some time and review what you have learned in today's study. What has the Lord shown you through His Word? Evaluate your own walk with Him. Are you spending time in His Word getting to know Him?

Reading His Word, praying and listening to the Lord are essential in order to grow in your relationship with the Savior. Be sure to set aside time every day to read the Word, to pray and to listen. Pray that He will give you a spirit of wisdom and understanding in the knowledge of Him.

DAY TWO

☐ Read Ephesians

Ephesians 1:18-19

1. What are the three things that Paul specifically prays for in Ephesians 1:18-19?

2. What is "the hope of His calling?" For additional insight, see: Ephesians 1:4-5; Romans 8:28-30; II Timothy 1:9. How do you think knowing the hope of His calling makes a difference in your day-to-day life?

3. Based upon the following passages, how would you describe hope that is centered on Jesus Christ? Romans 5:5; Hebrew 6:19; I Peter 1:3-5.

4. What are the "riches of the glory of His inheritance in the saints?" Use the following Scripture to support your answer: Ephesians 1:13-14; John 14:1-2 and II Corinthians 4:16-18.

5. How does the certainty of eternal life make a difference in your day-to-day life?

6. a. Our hope rests on the finished (past) work of Jesus Christ and our future inheritance is waiting for us in heaven. According to Ephesians 1:19, what is available to us today (presently)?

   b. What words does Paul use to describe God's power toward the believer?

   c. According to Ephesians 1:20-21, how is God's power demonstrated?

7. a. The same power that raised Jesus Christ from the dead lives in us through the indwelling Holy Spirit. According to the following, in what ways can we experience the surpassing greatness of His power? Acts 1:8; II Corinthians 12:9; Galatians 2:20-21.

b. How have you seen the power of God at work in your life? Or, in what areas of your life do you need to see the surpassing greatness of His power demonstrated?

Reflection

I cannot help but notice again that the emphasis of this passage, as well as the emphasis of the first three chapters, is Jesus Christ and what He has done for us. Before the foundation of the world we were chosen in Him. We were predestined to become God's children! Because of His great love and grace, we have been redeemed, set free from slavery to sin right here and now, and we have the Holy Spirit as a pledge of our inheritance. Every spiritual blessing in the heavenly places is ours in Christ.

Take some time to thank the Lord for the rich truths of Ephesians chapter one. Thank Him for choosing you, redeeming you and promising you eternal life.

DAY THREE

☐ Read Ephesians

Ephesians 1:20-23

1. Once again, read Ephesians 1:15-23. Looking specifically at Ephesians 1:20-23, what is the basis for our hope, inheritance, and power?

2. Why are the death, burial and resurrection of Jesus Christ central to Christianity? Use Scripture to support your answer.

3. According to this same passage, where is Jesus Christ right now? What kind of authority has He been given? Over whom and when is His authority exercised?

4. Read Philippians 2:9-11. What do you learn about Christ's authority in the age to come?

5. Once again, reflect on Ephesians 1:3-14. Why do you think Paul prays the prayer of Ephesians 1:18, 19?

6. Based upon what you have learned so far, why do you think being grounded in your position in Christ helps you obey Christ?

ⓔ Digging Deeper: The Word Study Process

As a new believer I was challenged to seek the Lord with all of my heart, soul, mind, and strength. Early in my walk with the Lord, the woman who was discipling me taught me how to do a "Word Study." The first word I studied was "seek," and it proved to be very insightful and encouraging to me in my pursuit of the Lord.

1. Select a word: When observing a text, select the individual words that are most significant to the passage's meaning or that appear interesting.

2. Look it up in a concordance: Locate the word in the main body of the concordance, taking note of the reference number. Using the reference number, locate the "original word" (the actual Hebrew, Aramaic, or Greek word) in the correct dictionary in the back (1. Hebrew/Aramaic or 2. Greek). Write down the definition assigned to the word, and take note of the various ways in which the word has been translated in English and which translation is most common. (The concordance should match the version of the Bible used.)

3. Examine the original word used in other texts: Look up other passages that use this same "original word" (same reference number), even though it may be translated differently in English. This can be done by looking up the various English translations of the "original word" in the main body of the concordance and noting those passages that have the same reference number. Develop an understanding of how the "original word" (same reference number) is used in these other contexts.

4. Consult word study tools: Look up your word in a variety of word study tools.

   Bible Dictionaries present immediate access to much scholarly information for everything "from A to Z." Look up the selected English word, and/or its synonyms if needed, and search out additional information. Note the transliteration of the selected word when referenced. (Revell's Concise Bible Dictionary, Holman Bible Dictionary.)

   Expository Dictionaries show how particular "original words" are translated in English, how they are used in different contexts, what theological ideas are possibly attached to a particular word, and Greek synonyms of each word. By utilizing a combination of the selected English word (or synonym if needed), the transliteration of the "original word," and/or reference number, locate the transliterated "original word" and its defined usage (Vine's Expository Dictionary of Old and New Testament Words, The Complete Word Study Dictionary—NT and OT).

5. Write out a summary of findings: Go back to the original passage and, based upon the general usage of the word, define the word in the light of the immediate context. Write a summary statement of the meaning of the word in this particular context. Remember, CONTEXT IS KING!

   For our study on the word "seek," I have chosen verses from my Topical Bible. I have not listed all of the verses, but have listed several of my favorites.

   Deuteronomy 4:29

   I Chronicles 16:11; 22:19

   II Chronicles 31:21

   Psalm 9:10

   Psalm 22:26

   Psalm 24:3-6

   Psalm 27:4,8

   Psalm 63:1-8

   Psalm 70:4-5

   Psalm 105:4

   Proverbs 2:3-5

Proverbs 28:5

Isaiah 55:6

Jeremiah 29:11-13

Lamentations 3:25-26

Matthew 6:33

Luke 11:9-12

DAY FOUR

☐ Read Ephesians

Luke 10:38-42

I love the way the prayer of Ephesians 1:15-23 teaches us about God's desire for us to know Him. It never ceases to amaze me that He really wants me to know Him intimately. He wants me to praise and worship Him, He has given me free access to the throne of grace and He has given me His living and abiding Word. One great thing about the Word of God is that it is full of illustrations. Not only are we given practical instruction, but also living examples to learn from. Today's study centers around a woman named Mary and her relationship with the Lord. She has always been a real encouragement to me as I grow in my knowledge of Him.

1. Read Luke 10:38-42. Who are the two women who are introduced to us in this passage? Describe briefly the scene at hand.

2. What is Martha's priority, according to Luke 10:38 and 40? What is Mary's priority, according to Luke 10:39,42?

3. According to Luke 10:40, what one word describes Martha?

4. Define DISTRACTION:

5. What things distract you from sitting at the Lord's feet?

6. How does the Lord describe Martha in Luke 10:41? Was it wrong for her to be preparing a meal for Jesus?

7. How do the Lord and this passage describe Mary? Use Scripture to support your answer.

8. In John chapter 11 we find Jesus on His way back to the home of Mary and Martha—this time because their brother Lazarus had died. Both women believed that if Jesus had come right away, He would have saved their brother from death.

   a. Read John 11:17-27 and 39-44. How does Martha respond to Jesus' arrival and His request to open the tomb of Lazarus?

   b. Read John 11:28-37. Record the differences between Mary's response and Martha's. How are they consistent with the passage in Luke 10?

   c. How does the Lord respond to each woman in her grief? What does this tell you about Jesus?

9. Read John 12:1-8 and Mark 14:1-9. In this passage we find Jesus and His disciples eating another meal together—shortly before Jesus is taken to the cross. Read this passage and record what you learn about Mary. Ask yourself such questions as: How is Mary's attitude and devotion different from those around her? How do their questions and accusations affect her outpouring of love? What does this tell you about Mary? What does this passage teach you about Jesus?

10. In Mark 14:1-9 a very interesting bit of information is added—can you find it? Look closely at Mark 14:9. Why is this included for us to learn from?

Reflection

Did you notice that in each instance referenced we find Mary at the feet of Jesus? She did not allow preparations to distract her; she worshipped Him in her grief and she did not allow others to dissuade her from simple and pure devotion to Christ. Who better reflects your life and attitude toward Jesus, Martha or Mary, and why?

Based upon what you have learned from these two women, what is the benefit of Christ-centered devotion and what would this look like for you? Pray and ask the Lord to give you the desire to make Him the Lord of your life, the One to whom you would give wholehearted devotion.

DAY FIVE

☐ Read Ephesians

Copy Ephesians 1:15-23 in the back of the book.

One of the greatest privileges of being a part of the birth of Moscow Bible Church was watching new believers learn the value of sitting at the feet of Jesus. Each of the men in leadership during those early years emphasized the importance of time in the Word. As Oleg now pastors the congregation, I am certain that the prayer of Ephesians 1:15-23 reflects his desire for the believers in his flock.

1. Take some time to pray. Pray for Moscow Bible Church. Pray for your pastor and your church. Pray Ephesians 1:15-23 for yourself, for your children, your spouse, or your disciple.

2. By way of review and reminder, go back to the TRUTH SEARCH found on Day 1 Number 6. If you have not looked up all of the verses, do so today. Pray that you will be one who boasts in understanding and knowing Him, that you would follow Him, and seek Him all of your days. Pray that everything around you would pale in comparison to knowing Christ Jesus the Lord. Thank Him that He has given you everything pertaining to life and godliness! Thank Him for giving you the desire to follow Him. Thank Him that the more you know Him, the more you trust Him.

3. Write out Psalm 73:25-28 and make it your prayer.

1 Kaul, 1998.

"But God, being rich in mercy, because of His great love with which He loved us, even when we were dead in our transgressions, made us alive together with Christ (by grace you have been saved), and raised us up with Him, and seated us with Him in the heavenly places, in Christ Jesus, in order that in the ages to come He might show the surpassing riches of His grace in kindness toward us in Christ Jesus."

Ephesians 2:4-7

LESSON FOUR

The Riches of His Mercy
Ephesians 2:1-10

Throughout the Fall of 1991, our strategy to begin reaching university students was to find those that spoke English. So we visited the English Department at Moscow State University, or faculties as they are called in Russia. Because of the fall of communism, the unstable economy, and the general uncertainty that seemed to permeate the country, many of the teachers and professors at Moscow State University left without warning. When our team arrived on campus looking for English-speaking students, we were immediately noticed and sought after. I remember one professor who not only asked us to teach some classes, but also, upon learning that we were Christians and knew about the Bible, asked us to teach Bible History to her students. She told us she understood that the history found in the Bible was significant not only in the past, but also in the present. Bob agreed to teach Walk Through the Bible to a class of English majors. Our routine was to go with him, listen to his lectures, and then break up into small discussion groups. As we would discuss the lesson of the day, we often had the opportunity to share the Gospel and to make acquaintances with students. One student particularly stood out to all of us. His name was Arteom. He was a 25-year-old student who spoke English very well. He had been a sergeant in the Russian army in Afghanistan shortly before our meeting.

He had terrible memories of his time in Afghanistan, regretted many of the things he had been part of, and clearly needed to experience the love and forgiveness that only Jesus Christ could offer.

Arteom and John, one of our team members, quickly became friends. Arteom told John that he was only attending the class for the purpose of practicing English and that he was not at all interested in Christianity. Of this he reminded John several times over the course of the Fall term. Little did he know we prayed for his salvation daily!

In late November, Campus Crusade for Christ sponsored a Bible Conference (one of many "firsts") for students from all over the Former Soviet Union. Students came from as far away as Kazakhstan and Kyrghystan, Lithuania and Georgia, as well as Russia. Several hundred university students, believers and non-believers, joined together to learn more about God and His Word. Due to communism, Bibles had not been printed in Russia for many, many years. We acquired Bibles from the Slavic Gospel Mission and passed them out to each student on the day they registered. The Bibles were about the size of a hefty phone book, but what a thrill it was to hand students their very first Bible! In addition to students from the republics I have mentioned, several students from Bob's class at Moscow State joined us, including Arteom.

I remember standing in the lobby of the hotel where the meetings were being held, talking to a few of my teammates when Arteom approached us. He told us that he felt himself "tumbling toward Christianity." He had terrible memories of his time in Afghanistan, regretted many of the things he had been part of, and clearly needed to experience the love and forgiveness that only Jesus Christ could offer. Eventually, Arteom "tumbled" right into the arms of the Savior!

There were many students who trusted Christ as their Savior that fall and at the Bible Conference. What a privilege it was to watch as the Lord drew them to Himself, and what a privilege it was to be a part of helping students understand the rich grace and mercy of God. As you begin this lesson, pray that you will grow in your understanding of the riches of your salvation. Pray that the Lord would "give you a spirit of wisdom and of revelation in the knowledge of Him." Pray that the "eyes of your heart may be enlightened, so that you will know what is the hope of His calling, what are the riches of the glory of His inheritance in the saints, and what is the surpassing greatness of His power toward you," His child.

DAY ONE

☐ Read Ephesians

Ephesians 2:1-3

1. For the sake of review, go back to Ephesians 1:3-14. Using one word for each, summarize our past, present, and future position in Christ.

2. Again, for the sake of review: For what purpose has the Lord chosen, redeemed, and sealed us? Use Scripture to support your answer.

3. Since the emphasis of Paul's prayer in Ephesians 1:15-23 is knowing the Lord, what have you learned so far about Him? Or, what has encouraged you the most about the Lord?

4. Ephesians chapter one emphasizes our riches in Christ. Record all the words and phrases in verses 3-14 that describe our riches in Christ.

5. Read Ephesians 2:1-3. After describing our riches, why do you think Paul takes us back to our condition before we were in Christ?

6. According to Ephesians 2:1, what was our "former" condition? Look closely at the text.

7. Read Ephesians 2:2-3. How does the text describe our walk before knowing Christ?

8. TRUTH SEARCH

    Read the following passages to enhance your understanding of man's condition apart from Jesus Christ. Psalm 53:1-3; Romans 3:10-18, 23; 6:23.

9. How does understanding our condition before Christ increase our appreciation of all that is ours in Christ?

Reflection

Over the years I have grown in respect and reverence for God. The longer I walk with Him and the more I meditate on the wonder of salvation, the more I am humbled. To think that I have passed out of death and into life. And it's not because of anything I have done but because of the rich mercy and grace of the Father, at times leaves me speechless. What about you? Have you thanked Him for giving you life in Christ? Never stop thanking Him! Have you taken the time to meditate upon the amazing truths of Ephesians 1-2:3? Read this passage aloud, and as you do, thank the Lord for all that He has done for you.

DAY TWO

☐ Read Ephesians

Ephesians 2:4-7

1. For the sake of review look again at Ephesians 2:1-3. What was man's condition apart from Christ and for what reason?

2. Look closely at Ephesians 2:4-7. In Ephesians 2:5a, what is Paul reminding us about man's condition?

3. a. Using your dictionary, define DEAD.

   b. What does it mean to be DEAD in our transgressions?

4. Ephesians 2:4-7 begins with the phrase "But God." In spite of our sinful rebelliousness, what did God do for us? What motivated Him to do so? Look closely at the text.

5. The definition for rich is "over abounding, without measure, unlimited." According to this passage, in what is God rich?

6. What does it mean to you personally to know that God has shown you His rich mercy and grace by making you alive in Christ?

7. One of the things I love about God's Word is that it not only teaches but also demonstrates the truths of God. We are going to take a look at a woman in the Gospel of John who illustrates for us the truths of this passage in Ephesians. Read John 4:7-18. How would you describe the woman at the well? Look closely and consider what she might have been lacking. What was her condition spiritually?

8. How would you describe Jesus and His attitude toward her and her sin? What does He promise her?

9. Read John 4:19-26. Notice how the woman changed the subject upon learning that Jesus knew about her numerous failed marriages and her current situation. How does Jesus bring the conversation back to her deepest need? What does the woman need to understand in order to receive life from the Lord?

10. According to John 4:27-29, 39-42, what did this woman do once she tasted the "water of life"?

11. What about you? Have you passed from death to life in Christ? Have you placed your faith in Jesus Christ to pay the penalty for your sin? If not, let the woman at the well be your example of one who found life and freedom in Christ Jesus. Place your faith in Him who is rich in mercy, great in love, and full of grace.

DAY THREE

☐ Read Ephesians

Ephesians 2:8-9

1. Remember that we began Ephesians chapter two DEAD in our trespasses and sins until God, being rich in mercy and great in love, made us alive together with Christ. Based upon Ephesians 2:4-9, what role do we play in being made alive? Look closely at the text.

2. It has often been said that our faith does not save us—the object of our faith does. The Word of God teaches that salvation is found only in Jesus Christ. Why is that true? And why is He alone worthy of our faith?

3. TRUTH SEARCH

   What is the "gift of God" spoken of in Ephesians 2:8 and John 4:10? According to the following verses, how is the "gift of God" described? John 3:16; Romans 3:24; 5:15-17; 6:23; 8:31-32; I Timothy 2:2-6.

4. a. Read Ephesians 2:8-9. Why does Paul emphasize that salvation is not by works?

   b. What is man prone to do according to these verses? Look up Romans 3:23-29 for further insight.

5. Consider the woman at the well in John 4. In what ways does she describe what is written in Ephesians 2:4-9?

6. a. What about you? Which category do you fall under, Ephesians 2:1-3 or Ephesians 2:4-9? How do you know?

   b. Based upon what you have learned so far, what must a person do to be saved? Use Scripture to support your answer.

7. If you were to die tonight, on a scale of 0% to 100%, how sure are you that you would spend eternity with God? If you cannot answer that question with "100%," then look again at Ephesians 2:1-9. Review Day Two and Day Three of this lesson.

In order to answer that question with "100%" you simply need to accept the gift of God, His only begotten Son, as your Savior. Place your faith in Him. Let His death pay the penalty for your sin, and thank Him that He chose you before the foundation of the world as His child, that He redeemed you, and that He promises you eternal life! Like the woman at the well, go tell others about your newfound faith in Jesus Christ!

Reflection

Let me encourage you, whether you have recently placed your faith in Christ or have known Him for many years, to pray for boldness in evangelism! All around us (in your neighborhood, your place of employment, or the classroom) are people who need to know Jesus Christ. There are people much like the woman at the well—bearing the consequences of their sin and thirsting for the kind of love and forgiveness only Jesus Christ can offer.

For most of my Christian life I have kept a "praying for salvation" list in the front of my journal. I frequently add names to that list, and from time to time rejoice when I can finally scratch a name off due to the salvation of that person! Make your own list, and begin praying for other believers to be bold witnesses in the lives of those you love. Pray you will be bold in your witness! Who knows? You may be the answer to another believer's prayers!

DAY FOUR

☐ Read Ephesians

Ephesians 2:10

1. Having studied Ephesians 2:1-9, what insights have you gained?

2. We have learned in Ephesians 2:5 that we have been made alive in Christ. II Corinthians 5:17 says: "Therefore if any man is in Christ the old things have passed away; behold new things have come."

    a. In Ephesians 2:10 what word is used to describe the person who is in Christ?

    b. Define that one word:

3. The Greek word for workmanship is "poiema" from which we get the words "poem" or "workmanship," as it is translated in this verse. Look up the following verses and record what it means to be the Lord's poem/workmanship. See Romans 8:29; Philippians 1:6; I John 3:1-2 for further insight.

4. According to Ephesians 2:10, in Whom are we created and for what purpose?

5. "The same power that created us in Christ Jesus empowers us to do the good works for which He has redeemed us. These are the verifiers of true salvation." 1 Compare Ephesians 2:1-3 with Ephesians 2:10. What differences do you observe?

6. Look up John 15 and read verses 4-5. Since bearing fruit is a picture of "good works," describe what we must do in order to bear fruit (Think of this in practical, everyday terms).

7. Look closely at John 15:7-12, 16-18. What does the fruit of abiding in Christ look like according to these verses?

8. a. Based upon what we have learned so far, is our salvation dependent upon good works? How do you know?

   b. What should be our motivation for good works?

9. a. How does knowing that you are God's workmanship change your thinking? What does this mean in light of your day-to-day life?

   b. What changes will you make, or what choices have you already made in light of this truth?

Reflection

We are not even halfway through our study of Ephesians, and yet already we have been inundated with the riches of God's grace. In my own walk with the Lord I have found that the more I understand God's grace, the more I want to obey His commandments and live a life that pleases Him. Equally motivating is the truth we looked at in Ephesians 1:15-23, that God not only wants us to know Him, but He also has given us the power to live our lives in obedience to Him! How could we *not* want to please Him in every respect when He has done so much for us?

Take some time and simply thank the Lord for seeing you as His workmanship, His poem. Thank Him for creating you in Christ Jesus. Thank Him for creating you for good works prepared long ago in which you are to walk.

DAY FIVE

☐ Read Ephesians

Copy Ephesians 2:1-10 in the back of your book.

Today I am going to give you two options for study and reflection. My purpose for both is to focus on the great mercy and grace the Father has for each of His children, and to emphasize what it means to be in Christ. In order to live victorious lives for Christ, we must continue to grasp and understand who the Lord Jesus is, and make Him alone the center of our lives. It is easy to live for Him when we spend time with Him in His Word, growing in our understanding of all He has for us. Please choose one (or both) options. Please do not hurry through this day. It would be easy to get caught in the trap of finishing the lesson just so you can say you are finished. However, that would defeat the purpose of this Bible study. Take your time. Bask in the richness of relationship with Jesus Christ.

Exercise One: Who I Am in Christ

Beginning in Ephesians, look up the following verses and passages and record who you are in Christ. Insert your name appropriately in each verse (we'll start with Ephesians by way of review—we will be reviewing these a lot by the way!) For example: Ephesians 1:3 "Cas is blessed with every spiritual blessing in the heavenly places in Christ."

Ephesians 1:4

Ephesians 1:7

Ephesians 1:11

Ephesians 1:13

Ephesians 2:6

Ephesians 2:7

Ephesians 2:10

John 8:31-32,36

Romans 3:22,26

Romans 6:6,11

I Corinthians 3:16; 6:19

I Corinthians 15:54-57

Philippians 4:13

Colossians 2:10

Colossians 3:12

I John 1:9

I Peter 1:3-5

II Peter 1:3-4

Psalm 17:15

There are countless other verses that describe who we are in Christ. Keep a running list of the truths you discover in God's Word as you study. Which truth ministers most to you today, and why?

Thank Him for everything that is true of you in Christ. Thank Him for rewarding you with the riches of His grace and His glory. Thank Him that everything is absolutely true and secure in Christ Jesus your Lord.

Exercise Two: Psalm 139

1. Psalm 139:1-6: Write out these six verses and insert your name appropriately. Ask yourself questions such as: What strikes you about the Lord in these verses? What do you learn about Him? What do you learn about yourself?

2. Psalm 139:7-12: Again, write out these verses. Consider the emotions that the writer is expressing here and why. Look for the things he recognizes as true about the Lord.

3. a. Do you think the writer is glad the Lord is everywhere he is? Why or why not?

   b. When have you experienced the same emotions? For what reason?

4. a. Read Psalm 139:13-16. Write out this section of verses and insert your name appropriately. What do you learn about the Lord?

   b. What do you learn about you, the Lord's creation (look specifically for adjectives that describe His creation)?

5. a. Compare Psalm 139:13-16 with Ephesians 1:3-6. How long has He known you?

   b. What does it mean to you to know that you are "fearfully and wonderfully made?"

   c. What times in your day or your week might this truth encourage you most?

6. Is there someone in your life that would benefit from looking at these verses? Who?

7. Psalm 139:17-22: Record these verses. What do you learn about the Lord's thoughts toward you?

8. What is the purpose of Psalm 139:19-22?

9. Psalm 139:23-24: Once again, write out these two verses and, as you do, make them your prayer. I love these verses because they express the desire of one who is growing in the Lord. What are the psalmist's specific requests?

10. With the whole of Psalm 139 in your mind, why do you think the psalmist ends on this note?

11. Why would these two verses be well worth memorizing? Why would the whole psalm be well worth knowing and memorizing for you personally?

Reflection

Thank the Lord for loving you absolutely. Walk back through this psalm and praise Him for who He is. Praise Him for His greatness; praise Him for His omniscience (knowing absolutely all things); praise Him for His omnipresence (being everywhere all of the time); praise Him as the Creator of everything. Praise Him for His omnipotence (being all powerful over all things). Thank Him for knowing your heart and your anxious thoughts. Thank Him for His Holy Spirit and His Word that convicts you of sin. Thank Him for guiding you every day.

1 MacArthur, pg. 62

"But now in Christ Jesus you who formerly were far off have been brought near by the blood of Christ. For He Himself is our peace, who made both groups into one, and broke down the barrier of the dividing wall, by abolishing in His flesh the enmity, which is the Law of commandments contained in ordinances, that in Himself He might make the two into one new man, thus establishing peace."

Ephesians 2:13-15

LESSON FIVE

Brought Near By His Blood
Ephesians 2:11-3:13

In 1986, we traveled through Eastern Europe on a summer missions trip. We crossed from West Germany into East Germany by train, and as we did so, it was as if we could literally see freedom turn into oppression. The Berlin Wall separated west from east, freedom from oppression for miles and miles. The strands of barbed wire that twisted and turned for miles across the top of the wall were a sobering reminder of the separation. Not many years after our summer in Poland the foreboding wall came down! You can imagine the jubilation that surrounded the literal destruction of that wall in 1989. I remember watching on television as young people sprawled all over the wall doing everything they could to break the wall apart. With the destruction of the Berlin Wall came the beginning of the collapse of communism in Eastern Europe and Russia, bringing with it a new promise of freedom on all fronts. It was truly a privilege to serve with many believers who took advantage of the new freedom and took the Gospel to Russia.

I wrote the following in my journal on December 25, 1991: "USSR ceased to exist, and Gorbechov resigned. Today the hammer and sickle was lowered and the Russian flag was raised." The collapse of the Soviet Union was never better expressed than that day in December, 1991. The red Soviet flag bearing the golden hammer and sickle had flown proudly over the Kremlin for 70 years, symbolizing a government characterized by atheism, deceit, oppression and destruction. Now it came down—along with the government—and the Russian flag was raised, symbolizing...what? Change certainly, and the promise of freedom. But amid the new excitement and hope there was much chaos and uncertainty about what the future held.

Amid the new excitement and hope there was much chaos and uncertainty about what the future held.

As I read Ephesians 2:11-22, I cannot help but think of those days in Russia. For us, the lowering of the Soviet flag represented the opportunity to take the Gospel to a country whose people had been forbidden to believe in God. We had the privilege of being some of the first believers to share Jesus Christ with students who had truly never heard. The wall—a physical and spiritual barrier—had been shattered.

In Ephesians 2:1-3 we learned that formerly we were dead in our sin. We walked according to the course of this world, we were considered sons of disobedience, and were by nature children of wrath. Our sinful nature was the barrier between us and God. The only One who could break the barrier was Jesus Christ Himself. In Ephesians 2:4-9 we learned that God extended His rich mercy toward us. He sent His Son to die in order to pay the penalty for our sin and give us the assurance of eternal life with Him.

Because of Jesus Christ we are no longer separated from God—the spiritual wall has been shattered! This is true for any and all who place their faith in Christ. Such wonderful freedom we enjoy in Christ. Stop, set down your book and pen, and give thanks to the Lord for His rich mercy and grace. Praise Him for giving you new life in Christ!

As we begin our study of Ephesians 2:11-3:13, we are going to find there was dissension among the believers in the early church. Differences arose between Jewish and Gentile believers. For as long as they could remember a wall of separation had existed between the two races, both literally and figuratively. "God sovereignly chose the Jews to be His special people. 'You only,' He told Israel, 'have I chosen among all the families of the earth.' (Amos 3:2) God chose the Jews not only to receive His special blessing but also to be a channel of those blessings to others. Unfortunately, Israel never fulfilled that calling. She preferred to condemn the Gentiles, rather than witness to them." 1 Now the two have become one in Christ—the only One who is able to bridge the gap between God and man, and between man and himself. In order for the church (the body of believers) to be a witness to the world there must be the recognition that all believers are "reconciled in one body to God through the cross." This was true for the Ephesian church, and it is true for the church today.

As you begin your study today, stop for a moment. Pray that the Lord will help you to concentrate and keep you free from distraction. Pray that He will help you see the centrality of Christ in the unity of the body of believers.

DAY ONE

☐ Read Ephesians

Ephesians 2:11-13

1. Look closely at Ephesians chapter two. Record all the things you find to be true of you "formerly." Looking for repeated words and ideas in Scripture helps us to recognize the emphasis of a particular passage or book of the Bible.

2. Ephesians 2:11 begins with the word "Therefore." A great question to ask yourself when you come to this word is, "What is the 'Therefore' there for?" And as you ask yourself that question, look back to the previous passage. Why do you think it is important to keep the previous passage in mind?

3. According to Ephesians 2:11, how are Gentiles described? Who are the "so-called" Circumcision? See Romans 2:17-27 for additional insight.

4. According to Ephesians 2:13-14,16,18, what is the main emphasis of this passage? Where else in Ephesians do you notice the same emphasis? Keep your eyes on the text!

5. What five things were true of Gentiles "before Christ" in Ephesians 2:12?
   a.

   b.

   c.

   d.

   e.

6. Whom is this an accurate description of today and why?

7. Looking closely at Ephesians 2:13, what is true of Gentile believers now? What has made this possible?

8. TRUTH SEARCH

We, as believers, are no longer excluded from anything related to God. We have been blessed with every spiritual blessing in the heavenly places in Christ. We who were formerly far off have been brought near by the blood of Christ. According to the following verses, why is the shed blood of Jesus Christ central to Christianity? Romans 3:23-26; Ephesians 1:7; Hebrews 9:22; I Peter 1:18-19.

Reflection

The fact that you and I have been "brought near" to God through the blood of Jesus Christ is incredible news! The God of the universe, the One who spoke the worlds into existence, has initiated a relationship with you and me. In fact, the Scriptures teach that He is "intimate with the upright!" Spend time meditating on the following passage, praising and thanking Him for drawing near to you, and for giving you free and ready access to draw near to Him.

"Since then we have a great high priest who has passed through the heavens, Jesus the Son of God, let us hold fast our confession. For we do not have a high priest who cannot sympathize with our weaknesses, but one who has been tempted in all things as we are, yet without sin. Let us therefore draw near with confidence to the throne of grace, that we may receive mercy and may find grace to help in time of need." —Hebrews 4:14-16

DAY TWO

☐ Read Ephesians

Ephesians 2:14-18

1. Read Ephesians 2:14-18 carefully. We already know we have been brought near by the blood of Christ. What do you discover we possess in Christ in the following verses?

    2:14-15

    2:16

    2:18

2. According to Ephesians 2:16 and Romans 5:1, how did Jesus Christ give us peace with God? To whom is the peace of God available?

3. Ephesians 2:14 brings to our attention another kind of wall, one which is both tangible and symbolic.

    "The barrier of the dividing wall alludes to the separation of the Court of the Gentiles from the rest of the Temple (of the Jews). Between that court and the Court of the Israelites was a sign that read, 'No Gentile may enter within the barricade which surrounds the sanctuary and enclosure. Anyone caught doing so will have himself to blame for his ensuing death.' This physical barrier illustrated the barrier of hostility and hate that also separated the two groups."[2]

Ephesians 2:14-18 not only reveals the Lord's desire for unity among believers from all backgrounds, but also further illustrates for us what it means to be in Christ. How did Christ establish peace between Jew and Gentile believers? In other words, how did He make both groups into one?

4. "Christ, through His death on the cross, forever broke down every dividing wall between man and God and between man and his fellow man. The greatest barrier between Jew and Gentile was the ceremonial law...the feasts, sacrifices, offerings, laws of cleanliness and purification, and all other distinct outward commandments."[3] Read Acts 15:1-10. How is this passage an illustration of this enmity?

5. What is true for both Jew and Gentile according to Ephesians 2:18?

6. a. According to your study today, what is the main point of this passage?

b. What sorts of things can cause dissension and disunity in the church today?

c. What can you do to help preserve unity in your church?

d. Stop and ask the Lord to help you to be a unifier!

Reflection

In Romans 1:14-17 Paul writes: "I am under obligation both to Greeks and to barbarians, both to the wise and to the foolish. Thus, for my part, I am eager to preach the gospel to you also who are in Rome. For I am not ashamed of the gospel, for it is the power of God for salvation to every one who believes, to the Jew first and also to the Greek. For in it the righteousness of God is revealed from faith to faith; as it is written: "BUT THE RIGHTEOUS MAN SHALL LIVE BY FAITH."

The great truth of the Gospel is that salvation is available for all who call upon the Lord; there is no distinction. Jesus Christ died once for all, the just for the unjust. Everyone who receives Christ as their Savior and Lord finds peace with God and among men, reconciliation, and free and ready access to the throne of the Father. Such is the picture of the church (the body of believers) today. Like the nation of Israel in the Old Testament, we as believers (the church) are to be markedly different than the world around us. Our lives should reflect the Lord Jesus Christ. Take some time and thank Him for His death on the cross. Thank Him for establishing peace with God and between believers. Praise Him for reconciling you to the Father and for allowing you to run to His throne of grace confidently.

DAY THREE

☐ Read Ephesians

Ephesians 2:19-22

1. Read Ephesians 2:19-3:13. According to Ephesians 2:19 and 3:6, what is now true of the Gentile who is in Christ? What is true of the Jew who is in Christ?

2. a. How do Ephesians 2:19-22 and I Peter 2:4-5 describe the household of God (the church/body of believers)?

    b. Who is the cornerstone and why? Use Scripture to support your answer.

3. a. According to Ephesians 2:21, what is the present condition of the "temple" or "household of God?"

b. How does Ephesians 2:22 describe the individual member of this "house?"

4. TRUTH SEARCH

   a. According to the following verses, what do you learn about being a "dwelling of God in the Spirit?" I Corinthians 3:16-17; 6:18-19.

   b. What does it mean to you to know that you are the temple of the Holy Spirit? Are there things in your life that keep you from glorifying God and that do not reflect the holy life to which you are called? How do your life and choices set you apart from the world?

5. We have gone from being dead in our sin, children of wrath, strangers and aliens, to becoming fellow citizens with the saints, part of God's household, fellow heirs and fellow members of the body, and fellow partakers of the promise in Christ Jesus. Stop and thank the Lord for His grace that saved you. Thank Him for drawing you near and calling you His child.

Reflection

I Corinthians 6:19-20 says, "Or do you not know that your body is a temple of the Holy Spirit who is in you, whom you have from God, and that you are not your own? For you have been bought with a price; therefore, glorify God in your body." Taking into consideration what you have learned in the first two chapters of Ephesians, what does it mean to you that "you are not your own," that you have been "bought with a price?" How does this knowledge affect the choices that you make? Be thoughtful in your answer.

Praise God the Father, Jesus Christ His Son, and the Holy Spirit! What tremendous truth is found in chapter two! Thank Him for making you a fellow citizen with the saints! Thank Him for Jesus Christ—the cornerstone of our faith and of the church. Thank Him for the apostles and prophets who are the foundation of the church and thank Him for His Holy Spirit who indwells every believer. Pray that, as a body of believers the world over, we would bring glory and honor to Him.

DAY FOUR

☐ Read Ephesians

Ephesians 3:1-10

1. Paul had been a prisoner both in Ceasaera and Rome over a period of five years because of his faith in Christ. Whose prisoner did Paul consider himself to be (according to Ephesians 3:1) and what does this tell you about him?

2. For what reason was Paul eager to preach the Gospel to the Gentiles? Look back to the previous chapter, and Romans 1:15-17 for insight.

3. a. As you read Ephesians 3:1-13, what is Paul's calling in life?

   b. How do his attitudes and actions now compare with his attitudes and actions before he knew Christ?

4. a. How have you seen the Lord change your heart and attitude as you have walked with Him?

   b. How have your priorities changed as you have walked with the Lord and why?

   c. What should you do if you do not see changes in your life, but want to?

5. "'Mystery' in the context of the New Testament means something God had not revealed until now. We would not have come to know about it had God not chosen to reveal it."[4] Look closely at Ephesians 3:1-7. What specifically is the mystery that Paul is referring to? Keep your eyes on the text.

6. Look at Ephesians 3:7-10. In addition to bringing the Gospel to the Gentiles, what else did God call Paul to do? For what purpose? (See comments and Ephesians 1:8b-12 for additional insight.)

"No one knew the full meaning of God's promise to Abraham that 'in you all the families of the earth shall be blessed' (Genesis 12:3) until Paul wrote: 'And the Scripture, foreseeing that God would justify the Gentiles by faith, preached the Gospel beforehand to Abraham, saying, "All the nations shall be blessed in you"' (Galatians 3:8). No one knew the full meaning of Isaiah's prediction, 'I will also make you a light of the nations so that My salvation may reach to the end of the earth.'" (Isaiah 49:6), until it was explained by Paul to mean the offering of the gospel of Jesus Christ to the Gentiles as well as the Jews (Acts 13:46-47).

Old Testament saints had no vision of the church, the assembling together of all the saved into one united Body, in which there were absolutely no racial distinctions. The clues they had in the Old Testament were a mystery to them because too much information was lacking. That is why Jews in the early church—even the apostle Peter (see Acts 10)—had such a difficult time accepting Gentile believers as being completely on the same spiritual level as Jews. And that is why Paul was concerned in this letter to the Ephesians to state and restate, to explain and explain again, that great truth."[5]

7. For the sake of review, what is the definition for grace? How does Paul describe the grace of God in his life in Ephesians 3:1-10? For example: Ephesians 3:2, Paul saw himself as a steward of God's grace.

8. Consider the kind of man Paul was before he met Christ. Why do you think the grace of God motivated him in his service as a believer?

9. Ephesians 3:8 says that Paul was called to preach to the Gentiles the "unfathomable riches of Christ." Based upon what you have studied so far, how would you describe the "unfathomable riches of Christ?" Use Scripture to support your answer.

Reflection

For me the most motivating factor in this passage of Ephesians is the example set by Paul. He was a prisoner of Rome, but considered himself a prisoner of the Lord. He suffered the loss of all things, yet counted them but rubbish for the sake of Christ. Before he came to know Jesus Christ he had hated the Gentiles; yet now he counted it a privilege to take the Gospel to them, and to endure hardship along the way. Paul was a man who understood the grace of God and the undeserved gift of salvation. We see his appreciation in his descriptive words, his humility, and his devotion to Christ. Oh, may we be men and women who see the privilege of sharing with others the unfathomable riches of Christ.

Thank Him for choosing you to be a fellow heir, a fellow member of the body, and a fellow partaker of the promise in Christ Jesus.

DAY FIVE

☐ Read Ephesians

Ephesians 3:11-13

Copy Ephesians 2:11-22 in the back of your book.

As we conclude this week's lesson, look back over Ephesians 2:11-3:8. We were formerly separate from Christ, excluded from the commonwealth of Israel, strangers to the covenant of promise, having no hope, and without God in the world. But now in Christ Jesus, we who formerly were far off have been brought near by His blood. Jesus Christ broke down the barrier of the dividing wall and brought unity among believers and reconciliation between the believer and God. We are all part of the household of God corporately and we are individually temples of the Holy Spirit.

1. a. Look closely at Ephesians 2:18 and Ephesians 3:12. What special privilege do we have as believers?

   b. Define bold:

   c. Define confident:

2. TRUTH SEARCH

    Look up the following passages. What do you learn about the Lord? What do you learn about prayer? Ephesians 6:18-20; Colossians 4:2-4; Philippians 4:6-7; I Thessalonians 5:17-18; Hebrews 4:16.

3. In Ephesians 3:13 Paul writes, "Therefore I ask you not to lose heart at my tribulations on your behalf, for they are your glory." Based upon what you have discovered in this passage, for what reasons had Paul endured tribulation? What was his attitude regarding his trials?

4. a. As believers we are to be "occupied with Christ," to keep Him as our focus. In light of Paul's example in these first three chapters, how would you describe a life that is "occupied with Christ?"

    b. What does being occupied with Christ look like for your life? Think specifically about your life, your financial choices, etc.

5. a. Look again at Ephesians 1:15-23. What insight have you gained into Paul's heart now that you have studied this particular section of Ephesians?

   b. Why do you think he prayed so passionately for other believers to grow in their knowledge of God?

6. What about you? Are you growing in your knowledge of the Lord? What truths have ministered to you or have challenged you in these three chapters?

Reflection

Praise the Lord for His rich blessings listed in Ephesians 1:3-14. Thank Him for His mercy that made you alive together with Christ. Thank Him for the surpassing riches of His grace shown in His kindness toward you in Christ. Thank Him for bringing you near to Him, for giving you free access to His throne of grace. Thank Him for the household of faith that is growing into a holy temple in the Lord; thank Him for giving the unfathomable riches of Christ to you. Praise Him for His wisdom, for His purpose, and for His Son—the centerpiece of our faith. Ask Him to help you to be occupied with Him.

1 Gilchrist, Sermon on Ephesians 2:11-13
2 Mac Arthur, pg. 77
3 Gilchrist, Sermon on Ephesians 2:11-13
4 Gilchrist, Sermon on Ephesians 3:1-13
5 Mac Arthur, pgs. 90-91

"For this reason, I bow my knees before the Father, from whom every family in heaven and on earth derives its name, that he would grant you, according to the riches of His glory, to be strengthened with power through His Spirit in the inner man; so that Christ may dwell in your hearts through faith; and that you, being rooted and grounded in love, may be able to comprehend with all the saints what is the breadth and length and height and depth, and to know the love of Christ which surpasses knowledge, that you may be filled up to all the fulness of God."

Ephesians 3:14-19

LESSON SIX

His Amazing Love
Ephesians 3:14-21

The Fall of 1992 brought much growth in the campus ministry in Moscow and in the congregation of Moscow Bible Church. What had begun as a church attended mostly by American missionaries and Russian college students had turned into a congregation of men and women of all ages, from all different backgrounds. It was very encouraging to watch the Lord cause growth both numerically and spiritually in the lives of the believers in the church. As more and more people trusted Christ it became increasingly apparent that the time had come to hold the first baptism.

For several Sundays Bob helped our pastor, Ronnie, interview each person who desired to be baptized. They asked each to share his/her testimony and to verbalize his/her reason for desiring to be baptized. Because the church met in a theater in downtown Moscow and because the Moscow River was bitterly cold, we had the challenge of finding a place to hold the baptism. After several weeks of searching, a swimming pool in the center of the city was designated as the location for the first baptism service of Moscow Bible Church.

> *As more and more people trusted Christ it became increasingly apparent that the time had come to hold the first baptism.*

I remember standing along the edge of the pool with about 40 others as the service began. We sang some songs together, which sounded beautiful as they echoed across the water. Then one by one each new believer stepped down into the water, shared his or her testimony, and was "buried with Christ in death, and raised with Christ in new life."

Bob assisted Ronnie because there were so many wanting to be baptized. The first Russian to be baptized that day was a young student named Anya. Anya had been in my Bible study for almost a year and had become very dear to Bob and me. It meant so much to us to be a part of her special day.

This past Fall, seven years later, Bob and I spent two weeks in East Russia. While we were there we had the opportunity to be a part of another baptism service. This time Bob baptized twelve women in a lake. Before he began the baptism, Bob had us all stand in a circle around the twelve women while they shared their testimonies. I could only understand bits and pieces of what they were saying, but the one phrase I understood all of them to say was, "And Jesus Christ changed my life."

In both situations it was amazing to me to watch these Russian believers, young and old, from all different places in life, make public their identity in Christ. The Gospel of Jesus Christ, as we learned in last week's lesson, transcends all boundaries! Russians were becoming, and continue to become, part of the family of God! This week we will be focusing on a small part of Ephesians that is brimming with wonderful truth for all who are part of His family. What a privilege it is to be called children of God!

DAY ONE

☐ Read Ephesians

Ephesians 3:14-15

1. Record how the surpassing riches of God's grace are described in the following verses in Ephesians:

   1:4

   1:5

   1:7

   1:9

   1:11

   1:13

   2:4

   2:5-7

   2:8

   2:10

   2:13

   2:14

   2:16

2:18

2:19-22

2. a. Why do the surpassing riches of God's grace move Paul to worship (Ephesians 3:14)?

b. How does knowing of the unlimited riches available to you make a difference in your own life?

3. Stop here. Put your pen down, and walk through the verses listed in question #1.

Bow before your heavenly Father and thank Him for blessing you with every spiritual blessing in the heavenly places.

Do you desire to know Him better? Pray the prayer of Ephesians 1:15-23. Thank Him for His Son who died and rose again on your behalf. Thank Him that His Son brought you near, and that because of Him you are growing in your knowledge of Him.

Are you experiencing difficulties in your life right now? Thank Him that He is always with you and that you have free access to His throne of grace at any time.

Are you feeling guilty for past sins? Thank Him for His rich mercy and His great love that made you alive together with Christ.

4. Compare the prayer in Ephesians 1:15-19 with the prayer in Ephesians 3:14-19. What are the specific requests found in Ephesians 1:15-19? What are the specific requests found in Ephesians 3:14-19?

5. What are the similarities in both prayers? What are the differences?

6. What do you learn about prayer from Paul's example?

7. According to Ephesians 3:14-15, every spiritual family in heaven and on earth derives its name from the heavenly Father. Look closely at Ephesians 3:16-21 and record and enjoy what you learn about your heavenly Father.

Reflection

Pray earnestly that the riches of God's grace will make a difference in your life, your attitudes, and your motivation.

Memorize Ephesians 3:14-21.

DAY TWO

☐ Read Ephesians

Ephesians 3:16-17

1. According to Ephesians 3:16, what is the first request Paul makes of the Father?

2. a. According to Ephesians 3:16, we need to be "strengthened" in the "inner man." What does this mean?

   b. What circumstances in your life remind you of your need for the Lord's strength?

3. Read II Corinthians 4:16-18 and record what you learn about the "inner man."

4. TRUTH SEARCH

   What is the critical element to being strengthened with power through His Spirit in the inner man? Romans 8:5-6; Romans 12:1-2; Colossians 1:9-10; Colossians 3:16-17.

5. What kind of attitude did Paul have with regard to the power and strength of God according to II Corinthians 4:7-11; 12:9-10; 13:4? How does this attitude differ from that of the world?

6. a. Record Ephesians 3:16-17a.

   b. For what purpose does Paul pray for the believer's strength to be found in the Lord?

   b. Think of a time in your own life when you turned to God because you desperately needed to be strengthened with God's power. How did He answer your plea?

7. If Jesus Christ is dwelling in our hearts through faith, then what should our lives look like? Look at Ephesians 3:19b and 5:18-20 for insight.

Reflection

In what condition is your "inner man?" Are you setting your mind on the things of the Spirit? Are you renewing your mind daily by spending time in the Word? Is the Word of God richly dwelling in you?

How does your life reflect the riches of your inheritance in Christ?

Have you allowed Jesus Christ to fill up every part of your life? What is holding you back from wholehearted devotion to Christ? Ask Him to search your heart.

Is there any sin in your life that needs to be confessed? Is there any nook or cranny of your life that you have kept to yourself? Or is there any area that you have not completely surrendered to the Lord? Jesus Christ wants to be the Lord of every area of your life, and He has demonstrated that by not only giving you new life, but also by blessing you with every spiritual blessing.

Let me encourage you to yield your life to Jesus Christ—every bit of it! Ask Him to fill you with all the fullness of God. Pray that your life will give Him glory and praise.

ⓔ DIGGING DEEPER

In Matthew 12:34b Jesus said "the mouth speaks out of that which fills the heart." Do a word study on heart. I have narrowed your study to Psalm 119 and Proverbs. If you desire to keep digging, follow the Word Study guidelines found on pages 56-57.

Psalm 119:2

Psalm 119:7

Psalm 119:10-11

Psalm 119:34

Psalm 119:36

Psalm 119:69

Psalm 119:80

Psalm 119:111-112

Psalm 119:145

Psalm 119:161

Proverbs 3:3

Proverbs 4:20-23

Proverbs 7:1-3

Proverbs 17:3

DAY THREE

☐ Read Ephesians

Ephesians 3:17-19

1. Read Ephesians 3:14-21. We have looked at what it means to be "strengthened with power through His Spirit in the inner man." What is the next request Paul makes in his prayer? See Ephesians 3:17-18.

2. Ephesians 3:17 describes us as being "rooted and grounded in love." Based upon what we have studied so far in the book of Ephesians, describe a life that is rooted and grounded in love. Use Scripture to support your answer.

3. a. Look at Ephesians 3:18 and 3:19. What seeming contradiction do you find here?

b. How do you think we can grow in our comprehension of the love of God that surpasses knowledge?

4. Take your time on this question.

   Based upon the first three chapters of Ephesians:

   a. How would you describe the breadth of Christ's love (whom does He love)?

   b. How would you describe the length of God's love (for how long has He loved and how long will He love His children)?

   c. How would you describe the height of Christ's love (how high does His love reach)?

d. How would you describe the depth of Christ's love (how far down did He reach to display His love)?

5. TRUTH SEARCH

    The following verses and passages further enhance the picture of the Lord's love. Read them and record your observations. John 3:16; 15:13; Romans 5:5; II Corinthians 8:9; Philippians 2:6-8; I John 4:9-10.

6. Why do you think that comprehending the incomprehensible love of Jesus Christ is what fills us up to all the fullness of God?

7. How can knowledge and comprehension of God's great love (which He demonstrated for you at the cross) make a difference in your daily life?

Reflection

Worship the Lord Jesus Christ who became poor that we might become rich. Praise and thank Him for loving you absolutely and completely.

Praise and thank Him for His unconditional love. Praise Him that His love is endless and perfect. Thank Him for wanting you to know Him and His love.

I have often prayed the prayer of Ephesians 3:18-19 for myself during times when I do not feel His love, or when I am not seeing His love. I also pray this prayer for women that I am discipling. Often I make a choice to take God at His word regardless of my feelings or my circumstances. Do you need to take these truths by faith? Tell the Lord! Thank Him for the never-ending, never-changing truth of His Word.

DAY FOUR

☐ Read Ephesians

Ephesians 3:20-21

The prayer in Ephesians 3:14-19 is so rich! What a bountiful prayer this is! It is incredible to think that God's love has been poured out within our hearts. We have been lavished with His grace and entrusted with His treasury. As you begin your study today, thank the Lord for His Word and for His love. Pray that you will have a soft and teachable heart as you spend time with Him today.

1. What has helped you the most as you have studied Ephesians 3:14-19 this week and why?

2. Are there circumstances in your life that seem impossible to you? Why?

3. Read Ephesians 3:20-21 aloud. Write down "He is able." What is God able to do according to these two verses?

4. TRUTH SEARCH

   I recently have had many reasons to ponder this prayer, and these two verses in particular. I have counseled several people who are in desperate circumstances, who feel far from the love of God. As a result, I decided to do a "truth search" and look up every verse containing the phrase "God is able." It is an enriching and challenging study. Do the same and record your insights. Daniel 3:1-18; 4:37; Matthew 3:9b; Matthew 10:28; Romans 4:21; 16:25; II Corinthians 9:8; Hebrews 2:18; 5:7; 7:25; Jude 1:24.

5. Now take a close look at Ephesians 3:20-21. One step at a time!

   a. GOD IS . . . From what you have learned from Ephesians, who is God?

   b. GOD IS ABLE . . . From what you have learned from your truth search and Ephesians, what are some of the things God is able to do?

   c. GOD IS ABLE TO DO EXCEEDING . . . Define "exceeding." Why is God able to do "exceeding?"

d. GOD IS ABLE TO DO EXCEEDING, ABUNDANTLY . . . Define abundantly. Why is God able to do exceeding, abundantly?

e. GOD IS ABLE TO DO EXCEEDING, ABUNDANTLY BEYOND ALL THAT WE ASK . . . If you believed this, how would it change your prayer life?

f. GOD IS ABLE TO DO EXCEEDING, ABUNDANTLY BEYOND ALL THAT WE ASK OR THINK . . . What are you thinking about asking the Lord to do? What does it mean to you to know He can far surpass even the things you think about?

6. a. Is there a limit to what we can ask of God? Think back to the Truth Search.

b. What kinds of things did God do?

c. What are you trusting the Lord for right now? In Matthew 9:28 Jesus asks a blind man this question, "Do you believe that I am able?" What about you? Do you believe that He is able?

7. Read Ephesians 3:14-19 aloud. Why are we reminded of the breadth and length and height and depth of the Lord's love before learning that He is able to do exceeding abundantly beyond all we ask or think?

Reflection

Praise Him for being able to do exceeding abundantly beyond all we ask or think, according to the power which works within us. Give Him the glory for His work in and through your life.

Is there something in your life with which you have not been trusting the Lord with? If so, take it to the throne of grace. Trust Him, the One who loves you with an incomprehensible love, to do exceeding abundantly beyond all that you ask or think. Thank Him by faith for hearing your prayer and answering according to His perfect will.

DAY FIVE

☐ Read Ephesians

Copy the third chapter of Ephesians in the back of your book.

1. If you have not done the DIGGING DEEPER for day four, do it today.

2. Catch up on your lessons if you are behind.

3. If you are all caught up, take today to reflect and simply meditate upon Ephesians 3:14-21. Make it your prayer today. Pray for someone whom you are discipling or someone who needs to be reminded of the long and high, deep and wide love of the Lord Jesus Christ.

> ### Tools For Digging For Truth:
>
> At the beginning of each day of study I have written, " Read Ephesians." Next to the statement there is a little bubble for you to indicate you have read Ephesians that day. As a young believer, I was advised to systematically select one book of the Bible and read it 50 times as I studied it. Thus, I would become very familiar with the content of the book before I moved on to another book. While the number "50" may seem daunting, let me encourage you to try this method of study at least this once. It has proven to be a rewarding method for me and for many others. You may be tempted to give up after the 25th or 30th time, but persevere—the benefits are worth the effort! If you have been reading Ephesians each day of your study you have already read it thirty times! Congratulations!

"I, therefore, the prisoner of the Lord, entreat you to walk in a manner worthy of the calling with which you have been called, with all humility and gentleness, with patience, showing forbearance to one another in love, being diligent to preserve the unity of the Spirit in the bond of peace."

Ephesians 4:1-3

LESSON SEVEN

Walk in a Manner Worthy
Ephesians 4:1-16

I love the first three chapters of Ephesians, which lavish us with the love and grace of God. We have read over and over about the riches that are ours in Christ. We have seen quite clearly that our blessings, our adoption, our redemption, and our inheritance have everything to do with Jesus Christ, and have nothing to do with us. In fact, if we have learned anything, I hope we have learned that we do not deserve anything from God. He chose us. He reached out to us. He delivered us. He loved us. He brought us near and gave us free access to His throne of grace. Jesus Christ is the reason we have a relationship with God. It is imperative that we constantly remember who we are in Christ as we move into the practical section of Ephesians, which deals primarily with our relationships with one another as believers. In fact, Ephesians 4:1 begins with: "Walk in a manner worthy of the calling with which you have been called." We are called God's children. We are part of His household; we are the dwelling of God! How we live and how we walk is of the utmost importance to the Lord.

How we live and how we walk is of the utmost importance to the Lord.

Ephesians is easily broken down into two sections. Ephesians 1-3 teaches us our WEALTH in Christ, or our position as believers before God. Ephesians 4-6 teaches us how to WALK in Christ, or how to put into practice the new life we have been given. One of the most profound lessons I learned during my three years in Russia was the necessity of filling my mind with the knowledge of my wealth in Christ in order to walk in a manner worthy of the Lord. I am sure the Lord had been showing me this truth for some time, but not until I left home and had everything familiar stripped away did I recognize more completely what it meant to walk with and represent the One who died and rose again on my behalf. In fact, my first four months in Moscow were most miserable! I was frustrated with myself, hated my surroundings, and wondered why on earth I had to live in such a difficult place! It seemed like nothing I had learned in previous years of ministry prepared me for ministry in Russia. Life and food were different; the alphabet and the language were different; the universities and ministering to college students were different. The Lord began to show me the first year that I was going to have to learn to walk by faith, to trust His Word, and to lean heavily on Him. Of course this was something I should have been doing long before I went to Russia! My husband, Bob, said to our team early on, "We have been used to a ministry based upon performance, and now we must get used to a ministry based upon faith." He was absolutely right.

By the beginning of our fourth month in Moscow, I was losing my joy, my perspective, and my strength. I cried out desperately to the Lord for help on January 1, 1992. I began doing a word study (just like the one I had you do in Lesson Four) on the word "joy." I fully expected to find verses that exhorted me to be content and start being joyful! But what I found was the matchless grace of God. I found that He was the source of the joy I was looking for. He was the one who would make me glad. I have Psalm 43:3-4 written in my journal, "O send out Thy light and Thy truth, let them lead me; let them bring me to Thy holy hill, and to Thy dwelling places. Then I will go to the altar of God, to God my exceeding joy; and upon the lyre I shall praise Thee, O God, my God." After writing out those verses I penned this in my journal, "Your light and Your truth lead me into Your joy. You are the One who makes me joyful with gladness. Your joy is my strength, and I find joy when I seek Your presence and refuge. It is plain and simple, I must fix my eyes on You and be intent upon You."

You and I stand in the grace of God. No matter what we do, our position in Christ is secure. His love for us will never change and will never grow cold. Nothing can separate us from Him or His love. In fact, we have been lavished with His love, rooted and grounded in His love! It is in light of this tremendous truth that we are called to WALK. Living in such a way that honors Him and brings glory to Him starts at the source—Jesus Christ.

As you begin today, pray that the Lord will remind you of His everlasting love. Thank Him for loving you as you are. Thank Him for giving you His Word to look at and read every day! Thank Him that He is there within the pages of His Word! Pray that your life will reflect and honor Him because of all that He has done for you.

DAY ONE

Ephesians 4:1

1. Read Ephesians 4-6. Write down every verse that mentions the word "walk."

2. According to these three chapters, walking in a manner worthy of the Lord involves our relationships with other believers. Why do you think that how we relate to each other as believers is so important?

3. As you read chapters four through six, what do you observe about the Lord?

4. What more do you learn about the Holy Spirit in these chapters?

5. Read Ephesians 4:1-3. What is the "Therefore" there for in Ephesians 4:1?

6. a. Define entreat:

   b. What does Paul, the prisoner of the Lord, entreat his readers to do?

7. TRUTH SEARCH

   To what is the believer called according to the following: John 15:16; I Thessalonians 2:10-12; I Corinthians 1:26;31? What words are used to describe the believer's calling in the following verses: II Timothy 1:9; Hebrews 3:1?

8. How do chapters one through three prepare you to "walk in a manner worthy of the calling with which you have been called?"

Reflection

It is easy to forget the grace of God, the love that surpasses knowledge, and move right into DOING. Do not forget or set aside the riches of God's grace! Praise Him for His riches that are yours in Christ Jesus. Thank Him that He will show you how to walk in a manner worthy of His calling. Thank Him that He has strengthened you with power through His Holy Spirit in your inner man.

DAY TWO

☐ Read Ephesians

Ephesians 4:2-3

1. a. According to Ephesians 4:1-3, what five characteristics are evident in the believer who is walking in a manner worthy of the Lord? How does each characteristic set believers apart from the world?

   b. Look up the following verses and describe Jesus Christ's humility: Philippians 2:7-8.

   c. What must we do in order to be like Jesus Christ in His humility? Matthew 11:28-30; John 13:12-15; Phil. 2:3-8.

2. a. What is the opposite of humility? Read the following and record what you learn about this kind of attitude:
   Proverbs 11:2

   Proverbs 16:18

   Proverbs 18:12

   James 4:6

   b. It has been said that "pride is behind every conflict." How do you see this to be true in your life?

3. a. According to I Peter 2:21-23 and Colossians 3:12-13, how would you define gentleness?

   b. Why is gentleness a characteristic of one who is walking in a manner worthy of his/her calling?

4. Read Hebrews 6:13-15; Hebrews 11:7 (Keep in mind that it took Noah 120 years to build the ark.), Hebrews 11:23-27, and describe how these men exhibited patience.

5. a. Define: "forbearance"

    b. What does it look like when we show "forbearance to one another in love?"

6. a. According to Ephesians 4:3, we are called to be diligent to preserve the unity of the Spirit in the bond of peace. What does it mean to "preserve unity?"

    b. Why does this take diligence? Answer this question with your own experiences in mind.

7. Looking back over these three verses, how does each characteristic build upon the other?

8. Why do you think these characteristics need to be true in our "inner man" before they can be manifested in our outward actions?

Reflection

"The exhortation to 'walk in a manner worthy of the calling with which we have been called,' has lifelong implications toward God and toward others, and should greatly affect our conduct. There is no higher calling."[1]

Based upon what you have learned from Ephesians 4:1-3, consider your conduct and your walk with the Lord. Does your walk with the Lord reflect your wealth in Christ? In other words, what would it look like for you, in your day-to-day life, to walk in a manner worthy of your calling?

Considering the exhortation of Ephesians 4:1-3, what difference would such attitudes make in your relationships with your parents, your spouse, your children, your roommate?

Thank the Lord for your wealth in Christ. Thank Him for the surpassing greatness of His power that strengthens your inner man. Thank Him for His Word that gives you clear guidelines and instructions for walking in a manner worthy of your calling.

DAY THREE

☐ Read Ephesians

Ephesians 4:4-6

Consider Ephesians 2:11-3:13. Jesus Christ broke down the barrier of the dividing wall between Jew and Gentile (refer back to lesson five). He made the two into one new man thus establishing peace, and reconciled them both in one body to God through the cross. Unity has been established in Christ. It is our duty, as we learn in Ephesians 4:3, to preserve the unity of the Spirit in the bond of peace. Ephesians 4:4-6 reminds us of the basis for unity.

As you read, look carefully at the seven features of "oneness" in Ephesians 4:4-6.

EPHESIANS 4:4

1. There is ONE BODY: Compare Ephesians 4:4a with Ephesians 2:14-22. Why is it so important we remember that, as believers in Jesus Christ, we are part of one body?

2. a. There is ONE SPIRIT: Compare Ephesians 4:4b with II Corinthians 3:16-17. What is true for every individual believer?

   b. Compare Ephesians 4:4b with Ephesians 2:17-22. What is true for the body of Christ?

3. a. There is ONE HOPE OF OUR CALLING: According to what you have learned in Ephesians, what is the unifying factor of the believer's hope and calling?

   b. According to Ephesians 1:13-14, what role does the Spirit play in the hope of our calling?

EPHESIANS 4:5

4. There is ONE LORD: According to Acts 4:12 and Romans 10:12, why is it essential that we recognize but one Lord?

5. a. There is ONE FAITH: "Paul is not referring here to the act of faith by which a person is saved or the continuing faith that produces right living, but rather the body of doctrine revealed in the New Testament. In true Christianity there is only one faith. Our one faith is the content of the revealed Word of God."[2]

b. With that in mind, why is it important that we spend time in the Word of God?

c. How does knowledge of the Word of God contribute to the unity of the body?

6. a. There is ONE BAPTISM: "Water baptism was extremely important in the early church, not as a means of salvation or special blessing but as a testimony of identity with and unity in Jesus Christ. Believers are baptized in the name of Jesus Christ."[3] For what reason is the believer baptized today?

b. Have you been baptized? Why or why not?

EPHESIANS 4:6

7. There is ONE GOD AND FATHER OF ALL: What do you learn about God the Father in this verse?

8. TRUTH SEARCH

   a. Look up the following and record what you learn about the oneness of God and its importance with regard to unity. Deuteronomy 6:4; Isaiah 46:9; I Corinthians 8:4-6.

   b. Continue your truth search, and record what you discover concerning the one God in three persons – the "Triune God" or "Trinity": Matthew 28:19; John 10:37-38; John 20:28; Acts 5:3-4.

   c. Why is the unity/oneness of the Godhead an essential element of the Gospel? Use Ephesians 1:3-14 to support your answer.

@ Digging Deeper

Unity has been established in Christ, but not without cost. Therefore, the preservation of our unity and oneness is essential in the body of Christ. This was on the heart of our Savior just hours before He went to the cross. Look closely and carefully at the prayer of Jesus as it is recorded in John 17. What did He ask specifically of the Father?

1. Whom was He praying for?

2. What did He ask of God regarding unity?

3. What did He desire the world to see as a result of this oneness? Let me encourage you to take your time.

Linger long over the heart of Jesus Christ. Never forget the fact that long ago He was praying for you!

Reflection

What have you learned through your study of Ephesians 4:1-6? Thank the Lord for teaching you more about Him and His heart.

a. In what ways can you preserve the unity of the Spirit in the bond of peace this week?

b. In what ways might you have interfered with the unity of the body? What can you do to remedy this erosion?

Pray that Ephesians 4:1-6 will be obvious in your walk with the Lord. Thank Him for giving you His Word and His Spirit.

DAY FOUR

☐ Read Ephesians

Ephesians 4:7-16

1. As we continue in our study of the "worthy walk," we are going to receive more and more specific and practical instruction. Ephesians 4:7-16 instructs us in the matter of spiritual gifts given us from God. Read Ephesians 4:7-13.

   a. Who has given us our spiritual gifts?

   b. Why is it important for us to recognize God's grace with regard to our spiritual gifts?

2. Look closely at Ephesians 4:8-10.

   a. What insight do you gain about spiritual gifts, and what are these verses referring to?

   b. Compare Ephesians 4:8-10 with Philippians 2:4-8.

c. Why does Jesus Christ's death, burial, and resurrection give Him authority to bestow spiritual gifts? See Philippians 2:9-11 for insight.

3. Read Ephesians 4:11 and record the different spiritual gifts listed in this verse.

4. According to Ephesians 4:12-13, for what purpose are these particular gifts given? Keep your eyes on the text. See Romans 12:6-8 and I Peter 4:10-11 for additional insight.

5. I don't know about you, but when I read Ephesians 4:13 I find myself longing to be the person described in this verse! Based upon what you have studied so far in Ephesians, how do we "attain the unity of faith, and of the knowledge of the Son of God, to a mature man, to the measure of the stature which belongs to the fullness of Christ"?

6. According to Ephesians 4:14-16 what is the result of being equipped and built up as an individual and what effect does this have on the entire body of Christ? Keep your eyes on the text!

7. Look back to Ephesians 4:14 for a minute.

    a. What characterizes the believer who is not growing and maturing in Christ?

    b. What causes some believers to remain as "children?"

8. Thinking about everything you have learned so far in your study of Ephesians, what advice would you give the Ephesians 4:14 believer? Use Scripture to support your answer.

Reflection

Every once in a while the Lord stops me short. He ever so gently reminds me of my call to "preserve the unity of the body in the bond of peace." This lesson reminds me that our unity as believers is a witness to the unbelievers who are watching. Oh, how easy it is to rebuild the wall that Jesus Christ demolished. How easy it is to seek to serve my own interests instead of the interests of others. Is this true in your life? Join me in praying that we will "speak the truth in love, grow up in all aspects into Him, who is the head, even Christ." Pray that as individuals we will be contributing to the growth of the whole body for the building up of itself in love.

Thank the Lord for His humility and gentleness. Thank Him for being patient and for showing you forbearance in love. Thank Him for the unity that is ours in Christ.

DAY FIVE

☐ Read Ephesians

Copy Ephesians 4:1-16 in the back of your book.

As I mentioned in the introduction to this lesson, it is easy to jump to the practical, day-to-day application of God's Word. Generally speaking, we want to "do something;" we want to "get going," "start walking." How often we get caught up in the walk and forget to find pleasure and satisfaction in our wealth in Christ. He has lavished us with His grace and surrounded us with His love! What great motivation for walking in a manner worthy of our calling.

Look again at Ephesians 4:4-16 and record every line that mentions the Lord Jesus. He is the reason we are called to walk in a manner worthy. Let us not forget to fix our eyes and our hearts on Him. Today I praised and thanked the Lord as I read through the first three chapters of Ephesians. I know that I have encouraged you to do so before, but do so again! And again!

Unload your burdens on Him.

Jesus said, "Come to Me all who are weary (tired) and heavy laden (without zeal) and I will give you rest. Take My yoke upon you, and learn from Me, for I am gentle and humble in heart; and YOU SHALL FIND REST FOR YOUR SOULS. For My yoke is easy, and My load is light." Matthew 11:28-30.

As I have prepared for this half of Ephesians, I have also been reminded of the work that is involved in preserving the unity of the Spirit in the bond of peace. In fact, I wrote a letter to a dear friend to clear up some misunderstandings; and just this weekend I was visited by another friend who came to seek forgiveness on some issues that took place during our time working together in Russia. You know something? It truly does take DILIGENCE! How refreshing it is when the body does work together, when we are all focused on Jesus Christ.

---

1 Gilchrist, Sermon on Ephesians 4:1-3.
2 MacArthur, pg. 130.
3 Ibid. pg. 130.

"But you did not learn Christ in this way, if indeed you have heard Him and have been taught in Him, just as truth is in Jesus, that, in reference to your former manner of life, you lay aside the old self, which is being corrupted in accordance with the lusts of deceit, and that you be renewed in the spirit of your mind, and put on the new self, which in the likeness of God has been created in righteousness and holiness of the truth."

Ephesians 4:20-24

LESSON EIGHT

Walk in Newness of Life
Ephesians 4:17-32

One of the things I love the most about getting older in Christ is the ability to look back over the course of my life. I love looking back and seeing how the Lord used a set of circumstances, a conversation with someone, a move, or a trial to teach me, to lead me in a new direction, or to challenge me to trust Him more. His past faithfulness is always a place to rest when I am faced with an unknown future or when I'm overwhelmed by His present goodness. That is where I am right now—overwhelmed by His present goodness. Let me explain.

There were about fifty Campus Crusade for Christ staff and students who arrived in Moscow in the Fall of 1991. We all stayed together in a dormitory for the first three or four days in the country for further briefing and training. I remember quite vividly the night some students from Moscow State University came to meet us. Anya and Luda were two of the young students I met that evening. They did not attend Moscow State University, but were students at a Teacher's Institute. They had become Christians the year before and had been involved in the ministry that was just getting started at Moscow State.

> *His past faithfulness is always a place to rest when I am faced with an unknown future or when I'm overwhelmed by His present goodness.*

In addition to their ability to speak English and translate for different members of our team, both Anya and Luda had tender, teachable hearts, and desired to grow in their relationship with the Lord. They also wanted to continue to learn how to share the Gospel with their friends and classmates. It was not long before they became a significant part of our team and our ministry, but even more importantly to me, they became disciples! Because they were young believers when we met, they needed training in evangelism and discipleship, and they needed to learn and grow in their walks with the Lord. They were learning what it meant to "lay aside the old self and be renewed in the spirit of your mind, and put on the new self, which in the likeness of God has been created in righteousness and holiness of the truth." I met regularly with each of them individually, and we discussed different issues in their lives, from their relationships with their parents to their attitudes and actions in school. We seemed to always talk about ways to communicate the Gospel to their classmates and friends as well.

I recall one time when Anya came to me wanting to talk more about sharing the Gospel. She had a real desire for her family to come to know the Lord, and she was going to visit them. We talked about being bold, relying on the Lord, and using His Word as she talked with her family. I remember being so encouraged by the depth of her desire to see her family come to Christ.

I also remember one particular instance when I had to talk with Luda about her attitude and responses toward others. We sat on some stairs at Moscow State University one evening and looked at passages in the Bible that deal with the tongue, attitudes, and actions. It was a turning point in our relationship, and due to her teachable heart, Luda listened and learned and grew in her understanding of the Spirit-filled life!

My relationship with Anya and Luda progressed over the next few years. We continued to spend regular time together in the Word and ministered together on their campus. Anya began and continued to share the Gospel with eagerness, and soon both her mother and her sister received Christ as their Savior. Luda began discipling a student who had trusted Christ at one of the outreaches on their campus and together they were used mightily by the Lord in many different ways.

There is so much I could say about these two women! As I look back over the past nine years I can see how the Lord has continued to cause growth in each of their lives. Both of them are on the staff of Campus Crusade for Christ and minister to university students in various parts of Russia. Luda and her husband Dave (an Englishman) are in the process of developing training materials for the new staff members in Russia, and they have two children. Anya and her husband Brad (an American) give leadership to the short term missionaries that come to Russia— teams of Campus Crusade for Christ staff and students just like the one Bob and I were on in 1991. And I just received a call informing me that Anya has just given birth to their first child!

I tell you about Anya and Luda because each is a testimony of the transforming power of Jesus Christ in a life. We all are! The Lord chose both Anya and Luda before the foundation of the world. He blessed them with every spiritual blessing in the heavenly places in Christ! They have been redeemed and given an inheritance, all because of the rich mercy and grace of Jesus Christ. Anya and Luda chose to walk in a manner worthy of the calling with which they were called, and they chose to lay aside the old man and put on the new. As a result, the Lord has blessed their obedience.

As you begin your study today thank the Lord for His faithfulness in your life. Thank Him for choosing you, redeeming you, and giving you hope. Thank Him for the ways He is changing your life. Ask Him to open your eyes and your heart as you study Ephesians 4:17-32. Ask Him to help you to lay aside the old and put on the new.

DAY ONE

☐ Read Ephesians

Ephesians 4:17-19

1. Reflect on the faithfulness of the Lord in your life. Record at least one way you have seen the Lord change your heart, your attitude, or your actions. Be specific.

2. What was it that prompted the changes in your life?

3. In what manner is the believer to walk according to Ephesians 4:1? Summarize what that looks like according to Ephesians 4:2-16.

4. According to Ephesians 4:17, what is the next 'step' in the believer's walk? (In other words, how is the believer to walk?)

5. What characterizes the Gentile's (unbeliever's) walk according to Ephesians 4:17-19?

6. What is the main reason that the Gentile's walk is futile according to this same passage? Where else in Ephesians do you find a similar description?

7. TRUTH SEARCH

   a. Compare the believer with the unbeliever in I Corinthians 1:18-31.

   b. What do you learn about God Himself in this passage—what is wisdom to God?

   c. What is foolishness to God? How does that differ from the world's view of wisdom and folly? See Isaiah 55:8-9 for insight.

d. What are some illustrations of this difference in the world around us?

e. In what ways does God use the foolish, weak and base things of the world for His own purposes? I Corinthians 1:18-31.

f. Who should be our focus and why?

8. Why do we, as believers, need to be reminded to "walk no longer just as the Gentiles also walk?"

Reflection

Praise the Lord for choosing you out of the world. Thank Him that you walk in newness of life because of Jesus Christ the Lord.

Are there areas of your life where you have allowed the futility of unbelief to creep in and steal your joy and purpose in Christ? Are there things about the world that seem to tug at your heart and pull you away from Christ? Talk to the Lord about these things. Thank Him for the truth of Ephesians 1:3-23. Thank Him for His power that lives in you and transforms you. Pray that you would be one who boasts in Him and Him alone.

DAY TWO

☐ Read Ephesians

Ephesians 4:20-24

1. Read Ephesians 4:17-24 and compare it with Ephesians 2:1-3,11-12. What was formerly true of you?

2. Ephesians 4:20 says "But you did not learn Christ (or come to salvation) in this way." In what way? Keep your eyes on the text.

3. TRUTH SEARCH

   According to the following, describe the "old self." What action is the believer to take toward the "old self" and why? Ephesians 4:20-24; Romans 12:2; Colossians 3:8-11; I Peter 2:1-3.

4. According to the passages you looked at in your "TRUTH SEARCH," why do you think renewing your mind is the key to putting on the "new self?"

5. a. Read Psalm 19:7-8,11-13. How is the Word described and what does it do for us as believers? For example:

The Law of the Lord, His Word, is perfect and it restores my soul.—Psalm 19:7a

   b. How have you seen the Word of God renewing your life, your mind, and your heart in practical ways?

6. From all that you have learned so far, why do you think it is imperative as believers that we make a daily, moment by moment choice to walk differently from the world? What specifically does this mean for you?

Optional Exercise

Over the years I have found my "new self" at war with my "old self." After receiving Christ as my Savior, I began learning to lay aside ungodly attitudes and actions. In time, I also started putting aside ungodly thoughts and desires. The Scriptures teach us that the battle we fight between the flesh and the spirit is very real, and that we will fight the battle until we go to be with the Lord. The great news is that the Lord has given us the unlimited power of His Spirit (remember Ephesians 1:19 and 3:16) and the everlasting truth of His Word to which we can cling as we keep our eyes fixed on Jesus Christ—our victorious Savior.

Hebrews 4:12 says, "For the word of God is living and active and sharper than any two-edged sword, and piercing as far as the division of soul and spirit, of both joints and marrow, and able to judge the thoughts and intentions of the heart." Because of the living and active power of God's Word, we are admonished to be renewed in the spirit of our minds. In order to be renewed in the spirit of the mind we must spend time reading God's Word! Not only so, but we also need to memorize Scripture. Psalm 119:11 says: "Thy word I have treasured in my heart that I may not sin against Thee." As the Lord pinpoints areas of your life that need to be renewed, memorize verses that apply to that particular area. I have memorized verses and passages that relate to the tongue, anger, forgiveness, and unity. I have also memorized verses that communicate the Gospel so that I am ready to share Jesus Christ with someone even if I do not have my Bible with me.

As the Lord points out areas of your life that need renewing, ask Him to help you memorize verses that will assist in laying aside the "old self." Write each verse out on a 3 x 5 card and tape it to your mirror. Keep a file of verses that you are memorizing and take it with you to work or to school. Work on memorizing over lunch or on the bus ride home. Mind renewal is a lifelong process and is well worth the effort.

DAY THREE

☐ Read Ephesians

Ephesians 4:25-32

1. Read Ephesians 4:17-32 to refresh your mind. Look specifically at Ephesians 4:24. How does this verse describe the believer?

2. According to Ephesians 4:24, what does the "new self" look like? How is this possible? Use Scripture to support your answer.

3. Look closely at Ephesians 4:25-32. As those who have been "created in righteousness and holiness of the truth," what are we to "lay aside?"

4. TRUTH SEARCH

   What do the following verses tell you about your new identity? Remember these things are positional truths, nothing that you do can ever change what is true of you in Christ. Romans 6:4-11; II Corinthians 5:17; Galatians 2:20.

5. While our position in Christ is 100% secure, we are called to live our lives in a manner that reflects our position. According to Ephesians 4:25-32, describe the actions of the new person in Christ.

6. What are the reasons given for Christ-like behavior in verses 25, 27, 28, 29, 30, and 32? Keep your eyes on the text.

7. Think carefully and record why it is so important that we, as believers, always keep Jesus Christ and the truths of Ephesians 1:3-14 in mind as we relate to one another.

8. For review, how are we to walk?

Reflection

Thank the Lord for creating you in righteousness and in holiness of the truth. Thank Him for calling you to lay aside the things that hinder your walk with Him, and thank Him for giving you specific instructions on how to walk in a manner worthy of His calling!

DAY FOUR

☐ Read Ephesians

Ephesians 4:25-32 cont.

Today we are going to look specifically at each verse in Ephesians 4:25-32. Pray and ask the Lord to give you a teachable heart and wisdom as you study today.

1. Ephesians 4:25: "Lay aside falsehood, SPEAK TRUTH, EACH ONE OF YOU, WITH HIS NEIGHBOR, for we are members of one another."

    a. Look up the following and record what you learn about the Lord's view of falsehood and truth:
    falsehood/lying: Proverbs 6:16-19

    truth: Proverbs 3:3-4

    b. What effect does falsehood/lying have on our relationships with one another?

    c. Why is speaking the truth in love important as we relate to believers and unbelievers?

2. Ephesians 4:26-27: "BE ANGRY, AND YET DO NOT SIN; do not let the sun go down on your anger, and do not give the devil an opportunity."

a. Look up the following and record what you learn about anger: Proverbs 15:18; 16:32.

b. When is it possible to be angry and yet not sin?

c. What instruction are we given for those times when we do become angry and why is this such good advice?

d. In what way can you apply this in your life?

3. Ephesians 4:28: "Let him who steals steal no longer; but rather let him labor, performing with his own hands what is good, in order that he may have something to share with him who has need."

a. Define steal:

b. What are ways that we might steal?

c. What are we to do instead of stealing? Why?

4. Ephesians 4:29-30: "Let no unwholesome (literally "rotten or putrid") word proceed from your mouth, but only such a word as is good for edification according to the need of the moment, that it may give grace to those who hear. And do not grieve the Holy Spirit of God, by whom you were sealed for the day of redemption."

   a. Look up the following and record what you learn about the effect of your words, both good and bad. Proverbs 15:4; 16:24, 28.

   b. Define edify:

c. Why is speaking with words that edify according to the need of the moment important when you are speaking with someone? Use Scripture to support your answer.

d. In what ways do we grieve the Holy Spirit with our words? Why do you think we are reminded of our redemption here?

5. Ephesians 4:31-32: "Let all bitterness and wrath and anger and clamor and slander be put away from you, along with all malice. And be kind to one another, tender-hearted, forgiving each other, just as God in Christ also has forgiven you."

   a. Write out Hebrews 12:15. What is the lasting effect of bitterness?

   b. How can a proper understanding of the grace of God keep us from being self-centered and bitter?

c. Taking into consideration the context of this passage, why is it imperative that we put away ALL bitterness, wrath, anger, clamor, slander and malice? For what reasons might we be tempted to hang on to these emotions and reactions?

Reflection

Read Ephesians 4:17-32 aloud. As you are reading, insert your name where appropriate. Ask the Lord to renew your heart, your mind and your actions. To Him be the glory forever and ever!

DAY FIVE

☐ Read Ephesians

Copy Ephesians 4:17-32 in the back of your book.

1. Look back over this week's lesson. Consider Ephesians 1-3, and remind yourself of your wealth in Christ. Why is it easier to obey the Lord and to walk in a manner worthy of the Lord when you are reminded of His amazing grace in your own life?

2. As you have studied this passage, perhaps the Lord has shown you areas of your life that look more like the "old self" than the "new." What action will you take to "lay aside" your former manner of life this week?

3. Based upon what you have learned from Ephesians, what advice would you give to a believer who desires to walk in a manner worthy of the Lord?

4. a. Over the past twenty years of my Christian walk I have found two things to be devastating and destructive in a believer's life: bitterness and an unforgiving spirit. What do you think is the main cause for bitterness?

   b. Knowing that a "root of bitterness defiles many" (Hebrews 12:15), how would you go about uprooting bitterness in your heart?

5. a. Is there someone in your life that you need to forgive? For what reason have you not extended forgiveness?

   b. Why do you think a clear understanding of the Lord's forgiveness toward us is so important when it comes to forgiving others?

6. Have you thanked the Lord Jesus for His unconditional forgiveness? Have you thanked Him for His loyal love and matchless grace? Do so right now!

Reflection

Pray through Ephesians 4:17-32. Thank the Lord for making you completely new. Thank Him for clothing you with the righteousness of Christ. Thank Him for giving you the power of the Holy Spirit to live your life for Him. Pray that all bitterness, wrath, anger, clamor and slander will be far from you. Pray that you will be kind, tenderhearted and forgiving toward others, just as God in Christ also has been toward you.

"Therefore be imitators of God, as beloved children; and walk in love, just as Christ also loved you, and gave Himself up for us, an offering and a sacrifice to God as a fragrant aroma."

Ephesians 5:1-2

LESSON NINE

Walk in Love
Ephesians 5:1-20

Over the three years that Bob and I lived and ministered in the former Soviet Union, we had the privilege of watching the Lord expand the borders of Campus Crusade for Christ's ministry on university campuses throughout many of the former Soviet Republics. We often traveled to different cities to spend time encouraging the short-term missionary teams, often speaking at retreats that were attended largely by students who had been believers for a very short amount of time.

At a retreat in the republic of Kyrgystan (in Central Asia) there was a mixture of new believers and non-believers in attendance. We left the city of Bishkek and traveled by bus up into a village that was nestled against a beautiful mountain range that borders China. The retreat was situated at the base of the mountains, and even in early October there was already a lot of snow, though the weather was beautiful while we were there! This retreat stands out in my mind not only because of its beautiful location, but also because of one certain student we met. He was a student in Bishkek and had received Christ just before the Fall retreat. I remember him because on the second night of the retreat, Muslim men from a nearby village broke into the building where our students were staying and beat this young believer until he was bruised and bloody. They made it clear that they were beating him because of his faith in Christ. I remember quite well talking and praying with the staff and students at the retreat following the beating. All of us were concerned not only because of his injuries, but also because he was just a few months old in Christ. I wondered if this incident would cause him to shy away from proclaiming his faith or walking with the Lord. He participated in the entire retreat and we never saw him again.

They made it clear that they were beating him because of his faith in Christ.

This Spring, nine years later, I had the opportunity to talk with one of the Americans who had been serving the Lord in Kyrgystan at the time. I asked her if she remembered the student who had been beaten up for his faith. She knew immediately whom I was talking about and went on to explain that he is currently working full-time in a ministry to college students in another city. She told me that the city he is in has a strong Muslim influence; nevertheless, he is very outspoken about his faith, and is known for being one of the leading male believers in Kyrgystan!

In the republic of Uzbekistan we met another student who had trusted Christ as his Savior not long before we were introduced. I remember being drawn to talk to him because his smile lit up the room! After introducing ourselves, we asked how he became a Christian. He explained that he had been raised in a very strict Muslim home. Most Muslims that we met and interacted with were Muslim by tradition, not practice. So this student was an exception. I do not remember the details of his testimony except that he told us that his "blood was Muslim, but his heart belonged to Jesus Christ." He also went on to tell us that several of his family members were Muslim missionaries. He explained that he would never be able to return home to his village because of his faith in Christ—if he did he would most certainly be killed.

Ephesians 5:1 says: "Therefore be imitators of God, as beloved children...." When we walk with Jesus Christ we are called to be just like Him, to follow in His steps. When we do, we will walk in stark contrast with the world around us. In Ephesians 4-6, we are called to walk in a manner worthy of the calling with which we have been called, to no longer walk just as the Gentiles also walk and to lay aside the old self, and be renewed in the spirit of our minds. The young believers I have told you about were identifying with Jesus Christ, and as a result they suffered persecution. Yet, because they understood their amazing wealth in Christ and were empowered by His Spirit, they chose to walk with the Lord and boldly proclaim the Gospel of Jesus Christ. They made a choice to be imitators of God!

Ephesians 5:2 goes on to say: ". . . and walk in love, just as Christ also loved you, and gave Himself up for us, an offering and a sacrifice to God as a fragrant aroma." The love that we are called to imitate is a sacrificial love, a love that gives without expecting in return.

"For the blessedness of receiving is not all God has for us: a new world lies beyond—a world of giving: a giving first to God in surrender, then to man in sacrifice."[1]

May we be men and women who are surrendered to Jesus Christ, willing to imitate Him regardless of the cost. As you begin your study today, ask the Lord to give you ears to hear and eyes to see His truth. Ask Him to teach you what it means to "imitate Christ, and walk in love, just as He also loved you."

DAY ONE

☐ Read Ephesians

Ephesians 5:1-20

1. For review, record the two descriptions of the Christian walk in Ephesians 4:1 and 4:17.

2. Read Ephesians. As you read chapter five, record the three additional descriptions of the believer's walk.

3. As we have learned, Ephesians chapters one through three have to do with the wealth of the believer, and chapters four through six have to do with the walk of the believer. However, throughout chapters four through six we continue to be reminded of our wealth in Christ. Record each of the following verses describing our walk and the corresponding verses describing our wealth:

   a. Ephesians 4:24   Ephesians 2:10

   b. Ephesians 4:30   Ephesians 1:13

   c. Ephesians 4:29-32   Ephesians 1:7-8

4. a. Practically speaking, as you live your life day by day, why is it helpful for you to be reminded of your wealth in Christ?

b. Record practical steps you can take in order to keep Christ as the center of your life.

c. What happens when you do not keep Him as the center?

5. Based upon what you learned in Ephesians 1-3, what assurance do you have to fall back on when the walk of the believer seems to be more than you can handle? See Ephesians 1:18-20 and Ephesians 3:16 for insight.

6. TRUTH SEARCH

a. According to the following, how did Jesus Christ demonstrate complete dependence upon the heavenly Father? John 5:19, 30; 12:49-50; I Peter 2:21-24.

b. Ephesians 5:1 tells us to be "imitators of God as beloved children." What do you learn from Christ's example of dependence on His Father?

c. Why would you and I need to be much more dependent upon Him, relying on His power for victorious walking?

Reflection

Over the years I have encountered many believers who are not walking with the Lord or are not experiencing the joy of walking with Him. They have often completely forgotten, or maybe never even known what it means to be in Christ. For some, walking with the Lord entails not ever doing anything wrong and trying as hard as possible to do everything right, bringing sure defeat. For others, their slide back was a gradual one, and eventually their sinful choices created a distance between them and God that seemed impossible to bridge. It has been a real joy to take such believers back to the cross where Jesus Christ died for them and rose again to conquer sin. I have not shared anything new; I simply have shown them their wealth in Christ. As they have learned their position in Christ afresh, they have had an increased desire to walk with Him and serve Him.

We all have bad days and face times in our lives when we do not feel like the Lord loves us. We know we are not worthy of His love. Many times we do not know how to trust Him or we do not want to depend on Him. It is in those moments we need most to turn our eyes upon Jesus. May we never tire of hearing that Jesus Christ died on the cross to pay the penalty for our sins. May we never forget His incredible display of love. May His love compel us to be imitators of Him. May we learn to walk in love, just as He also loved us and gave Himself up for us. Praise Him for offering Himself up to God as a sacrifice and a fragrant aroma.

DAY TWO

☐ Read Ephesians

Ephesians 5:1-6

1. Read Ephesians 5:1-2. What is the "therefore" there for in Ephesians 5:1?

2. In what ways are we called to imitate God according to Ephesians 4:32-5:2?

3. a. Why is the Lord's forgiveness a display of sacrificial love?

    b. In what ways do you find forgiveness to be a display of sacrificial love in your relationships?

c. Why does God call us to imitate Him in this way?

4. a. Read I Peter 2:18-24. What kind of example did Jesus Christ set for us?

   b. Based upon what you have learned in Ephesians, what must you rely upon in order to follow Christ's example? Use Scripture to support your answer.

5. a. Read Ephesians 5:3-6. As we follow Christ's example, what are we to avoid in our speech and why?

   b. How do these verses relate to Ephesians 4:29?

6. Compare Ephesians 5:3-6 with Ephesians 2:1-3. Who are we imitating if we are "allowing these things to be named among us?"

7. Considering this same passage, what kinds of words are "proper and fitting among the saints?" Why?

8. a. What should our response be toward those who are immoral, impure, covetous, and idolaters? Why? Use Ephesians 4:17-5:6 to support your answer.

   b. To whom can we expose the sons of disobedience?

   c. Pray for the unbelievers in your life. Pray that Christ will shine His light in their dark hearts!

Reflection

Think specifically about situations or conversations in your life where you need to apply the instructions of Ephesians 5:1-6. Pray, asking the Lord to control your tongue. Pray your mouth will be filled with thanksgiving, with the truth of the Gospel, with the wisdom that is from above!

Jesus, while rebuking the religious Pharisees of His day, said in Matthew 12:34, "You brood of vipers, how can you, being evil, speak what is good? For the mouth speaks out of that which fills the heart." This is so true! If we, as believers, are filling our minds and hearts with the things of the Lord, and with the words from His book, our hearts will be filled with Him! Conversely, if we are filling our minds and hearts with the things of the world, our words will reflect the same. How important it is to be spending time every day seated at the feet of our Savior. Thank Him today! Fill your heart with His Word, His truth! As a godly Bible teacher once said, "Sit at the feet of Jesus and tell others what you see."

DAY THREE

☐ Read Ephesians

Ephesians 5:7-14

1. For review, write down the three descriptions of the believer's walk found in Ephesians 4:1, 17; 5:2.

2. Read Ephesians 5:7-14.

    a. Who were we formerly and where else in Ephesians do we learn about our former position?

    b. Why do you think the Bible reminds us about our former standing before God so often?

3. a. According to Ephesians 5:8-10, who are we now? How are we to walk?

b. What is the fruit of walking in the light? Keep your eyes on the text.

c. Why do you think "goodness, righteousness and truth" prove you are a child of God? Use Scripture to support your answer.

4. TRUTH SEARCH

a. Remembering that we are called to be "imitators of God as beloved children," look up the following verses and record what you learn about Jesus Christ: John 1:7; 8:12; 12:46.

b. Look up the following verses and record what you learn about walking in the light: I Thessalonians 5:2-8; I Peter 2:9; I John 1:5-7; 2:8-11.

5. a. According to Ephesians 5:8-12, why is the believer not to participate in or speak of the unfruitful deeds of darkness?

b. In what ways do we, as believers, tend to compromise in this area?

6. a. What positive steps can we take when we are confronted by those who are participating in the deeds of darkness?

b. To whom can we introduce the unbelievers in our lives? Use Scripture to support your answer.

Tools for Digging for Truth:

In the New American Standard Bible, Ephesians 5:10 says, "trying to learn what is pleasing to the Lord." This verse implies a "struggle," or an unending attempt to figure out what pleases God. However, this does not make sense if we believe Ephesians 1-3. We have already learned that we are powerless apart from Christ! Whenever you come upon a verse or passage that seems contradictory, or does not make sense to you, follow these simple steps:

- Identify the meaning in context. First, look at the paragraph in which the passage is found. The most important meaning of the verse is found in its surrounding paragraph. Second, look at the context of the entire book that you are studying. How does this verse relate to the theme, and outline of the book? Third, consider the verse in the context of the entire Bible. The Word of God, though diverse in its authorship, has continuity in its message. Remember, CONTEXT IS KING!

NOW YOU TRY IT! Look at Ephesians 5:10 by identifying its meaning in context. What do you learn?

- Let Scripture interpret Scripture. The best commentary on the Bible is the Bible itself. Use clear passages to interpret the unclear. Since God is the sole author of Scripture, what is taught in one passage cannot contradict what is taught in another. And it is important to remember that the Bible is an inspired whole that has one marvelous and supernatural unity.

Tools for Interpretation:

1. Cross-references: A great way of locating Scriptural passages is to refer to the marginal reference system in your Bible.

2. Concordance: Look up key words in a concordance and locate other occurrences of that word.

3. Treasury of Scripture Knowledge: This helpful book provides excellent cross-reference material and is easy to use.

4. Vine's Expository Dictionary of New Testament Words: This dictionary gives the Greek definition for every word in the New Testament, which can enhance your study, and help your interpretation.

5. Other reliable translations and paraphrases of the Bible: I enjoy the Phillips Translation because it offers clear, yet simple meaning.

> **NOTES ON HERMENEUTICS**[2]
>
> For Ephesians 5:10 I looked up the word "trying" in the Vines Dictionary. I learned that this word carries with it the idea of testing or proving. A good cross-reference is Romans 12:2. I also was encouraged by the Phillips translation:
>
> *"Have nothing to do with men like that——once you were 'darkness' but now you are 'light.' Live then as children of the light. The light produces in men quite the opposite of sins like these —everything that is wholesome and good and true. Let your lives be living proofs of the things which please God."*

Reflection and Call to Action

John MacArthur writes, "Light is that which makes things manifest, that which shows them to be as they actually are. When sin is revealed, it loses its 'hiddenness' and is seen for the ugliness it is."[3] Ephesians has reminded us that each and every believer was formerly darkness, but now as children of light we have the distinct privilege of proclaiming the 'Light of the World' to those in darkness all around us.

Ephesians 5:14 offers an invitation for those who are not children of God. "Awake sleeper" describes the sinner who is asleep in the darkness of sin and unaware of his lost condition and tragic destiny. Like a spiritual Rip Van Winkle, he will sleep through God's time of grace unless someone awakens him. Arise from the dead is a summons to repentance, an appeal to turn away from the dead ways of sin. Christ will shine on you is the good news that God has provided a remedy for every sinful person who will come to Him through His blessed Son, the Savior of mankind."[3]

Take time today to thank the Lord for shining His light on your life, for rescuing you from your former manner of life, for saving you and giving you eternal life. Make a list of people around you who are participating in the unfruitful deeds of darkness. Pray to the Lord for their salvation. Pray that they will awaken and arise from the dead; pray that Christ will shine upon them. Ask the Lord to use you to shed the "Light of the world" on their lives! Pray that your way of life will be "living proof of the things which please God," and that your words will be full of the truth of Jesus Christ.

DAY FOUR

☐ Read Ephesians

Ephesians 5:15-20

1. Record each of the descriptions of the believer's walk according to what we have studied so far. You should be able to find four.

2. a. Read Ephesians 5:15-21. What is the "therefore" there for in Ephesians 5:15? Consider not only Ephesians 5:14, but also 5:1.

   b. How is the believer to walk according to Ephesians 5:15?

3. a. Look carefully at Ephesians 5:15-18. What three things is the believer told not to do?

b. Look again carefully at Ephesians 5:15-18. What four things is the believer told to do? What reasons are given?

4. What do you think is the key ingredient to "understanding what the will of the Lord is" and "being filled with the Spirit?" Use Scripture to support your answer.

Optional Exercise

Read Proverbs 2. As you are reading, record the words that describe the effort made toward wisdom. For example:

"My son, if you will receive my sayings, and treasure my commandments within you . . ."—Proverbs 2:1

Next record the fruit or result of your pursuing wisdom. For example: ". . . Then you will discern the fear of the Lord, and discover the knowledge of God."

- What will wisdom guard you from according to this passage?

- What is the destination of the way of wisdom? What is the end of the wicked?

- What can you do to ensure that you are being careful as you walk? Think about your life, your day-to-day activities, your relationships both at home and away. Ask yourself the following questions:

- What am I doing to ensure that I am careful in my walk with the Lord?

- How can I guard against the temptations of the world?

- What have I done that has helped me stand firm?

5. a. How is the Spirit-filled life described in Ephesians 5:18-21?

   b. Compare this passage with Colossians 3:12-16. What are we to be filled with according to Colossians 3:16?

   c. Why does filling your mind with the truth of God's Word ensure that you are filled with the Spirit, and vise versa?

6. a. According to Galatians 5:22-23, what is the fruit of the Spirit?

b. Where in Ephesians have you found very similar descriptions?

7. Take some time to consider what you have learned in this week's lesson. How have you made, or how might you make, Ephesians 5:15-21 practical in your life? Think about a situation at work that is causing you frustration. Maybe you are a student and you are the only Christian in your study group. Maybe you are a wife with small children at home, or a husband having to work long hours. How will you take what you have learned and apply it in your life this week?

8. Are you discipling a younger believer? What have you learned this week that you can pass on to one who desires to grow in his/her walk with the Lord?

Reflection

In both Ephesians 5:4 and 5:20 we are admonished to give thanks. In fact, in Ephesians 5:20 we are told to "always give thanks for all things." Why is this so important? What if we do not feel thankful?

Thank the Lord right now for everything you can think of! If you are not sure where to start, begin by looking back over Ephesians chapter five. Thank Him for loving you; thank Him for giving Himself for you. Thank Him for your wealth in Christ. Thank Him for His power and strength . . . and so on!

DAY FIVE

☐ Read Ephesians

Copy Ephesians 5:1-21 in the back of your book.

We have been looking at and thinking about the walk of the believer. We have learned that we are to walk in a manner worthy of the calling with which we have been called, walk no longer just as the Gentiles also walk, imitate the Lord by walking in love, walk as children of light, walk carefully and walk wisely. Without a Christ-centered perspective that comes from being filled with the Spirit and Word of God, the walk of the believer would seem absolutely impossible!

Today simply read Ephesians aloud. Slowly and carefully read each word and verse and chapter with your own heart and life in mind. As you remind yourself of your limitless, priceless wealth in Christ, praise Him for choosing you before the foundation of the world, for choosing you out of your "former" condition!

Linger long over the verses that drip with rich expressions of His AMAZING love, grace and mercy. Do not skim over the prayers of Ephesians 1:18-21 and Ephesians 3:14-21—remember to pray for yourself and others in your life. Let the breadth and length and height and depth of the Savior's love for you be your confidence as you move through chapters four through six.

Thank the Lord that He has strengthened you with power through His Spirit in your inner man to help you walk with Him. Thank Him that He lives in you and walks with you. Thank Him for His Word and His Spirit that gives guidance and wisdom. Ask Him to give you an insatiable desire for His Word. Ask Him to bear the fruit of righteousness, goodness, and truth in your life. Thank Him for His patience and His everlasting love.

1 Huffman Rockness, page 43.
2 Kaul, 1998.
3 Mac Arthur, pg. 213.

"Slaves, be obedient to those who are your masters according to the flesh, with fear and trembling, in the sincerity of your heart, as to Christ; not by way of eyeservice, as men-pleasers, but as slaves of Christ, doing the will of God from the heart."

Ephesians 6:5-6

LESSON TEN

Walk in Obedience

Ephesians 5:21-6:9

Weddings are joyful events no matter where in the world they take place, and Moscow was no exception. Quite often we would see a bride and groom being photographed at Red Square standing in front of St. Basil's cathedral, or at scenic spots along the Moscow River. The bride would be dressed in white, the groom in a dark colored suit. In the winter we could easily spot a bride, her white veil streaming out from underneath her big fur hat.

Under the Soviet system of government, God played no part in marriage. In fact, getting married involved little more than an official stamp on a government document. In order to be officially married, the couple had to file an application for marriage at the appropriate government office. At that time they were given a certificate that allowed them to shop at a special store for engaged couples where, if necessary, they could rent a dress and suit. After a one month waiting period, the couple would be assigned a date and time for their marriage ceremony. On their assigned date, the couple would arrive dressed as bride and groom, with their passports and at least two people as witnesses. The couple and their wedding party would wait in line at the appropriate office.

> *Under the Soviet system of government, God played no part in marriage. In fact, getting married involved little more than an official stamp on a government document.*

Music would be playing as each couple entered the room where they would be pronounced man and wife. Before the official proceedings would begin, the couple would pay a fee, and then the master of ceremonies would invite the wedding party in to stand behind the couple. He would say a few words about the privilege of being married, the importance of commitment, and the ceremony would end in just a few short minutes. The couple would then sign more papers, give each other flowers, and leave as the next couple would step into the room. Afterward they would go around the city taking pictures and celebrating. Oftentimes there would be a meal presented either at a restaurant or the bride's home on the day of the wedding, and there would be another meal for all the friends and family the day following the wedding.

In the Spring of 1994, our Russian friend Anya and our American friend Brad aounced their engagement. They planned their wedding for July of the same year. It was exciting to know that their wedding and their marriage would be centered around the Lord Jesus Christ! Yes, they had to go through all the steps under Russian law to make their marriage legal in that country, but more importantly they made solemn vows before the Lord that day in July. (Anya and Brad were the first of our ministry in Russia to be married not just in a civil ceremony, but before God and His witnesses.)

One year later our Russian friend Luda and our British friend Dave were engaged, and their wedding took place in June of 1995. Though unable to attend their wedding, I had the privilege of sending Luda a wedding dress, shoes, a veil, and jewelry to wear on her wedding day! Since then Jesus Christ has brought many couples together who were part of the ministry we were involved in. What a joy to see young couples serving the Lord together, making Jesus Christ the center of their marriage and home.

As we will find in our study of Ephesians 5:21-6:9, when Jesus Christ is the center of our lives we will experience rich relationships with our spouses, our children, and our co-workers. What blessing there is in knowing that we have the Word of God to give us wisdom and understanding in every area of our lives!

DAY ONE

☐ Read Ephesians

Ephesians 5:21

1. Record each of the different ways the believer is to walk with the Lord.

2. Which description of the believer's walk has challenged you the most and why?

3. Read Ephesians 5:15-21. For review, describe the life that is filled with the Spirit.

4. Why do you think that thanksgiving is emphasized in this passage?

5. Look closely at Ephesians 5:21. What one word describes the attitude we are to have toward one another, and why do you think "in the fear of Christ" should motivate us to be obedient?

6. TRUTH SEARCH

   a. Compare Ephesians 5:21 with I Peter 2:13-24. Record each situation in the I Peter passage that requires a submissive attitude, and pay close attention to the reason given for submission.

   b. Whose example are we to follow?

   c. What words describe the Lord's submissive spirit? See Philippians 2:5-8 for insight.

7. Describe a time in your life when you had to make a choice to follow Christ's example in submission. How did your attitude affect those around you? Was it hard or easy? What was the end result? What else do you recall about the situation?

8. a. Why do you think a submissive attitude in any or all of these situations marks the believer out as different from the world?

b. List some of the reasons the world hates submission.

9. Is there an area in your life where you need to make the choice to "be subject to one another in the fear of Christ?" What specifically do you need to do in order to be submissive?

Reflection

Throughout chapters four and five, we have heard clear instruction in how to walk in a way that gives glory to the Lord. Much of our walk with God concerns our relationships with one another as believers. "Be diligent to preserve the unity of the spirit in the bond of peace," "speak truth each one of you with his neighbor, for we are members of one another," and "be subject to one another in the fear of Christ" are just a few of the admonitions given in Ephesians. Remember that we are to be imitators of God! We are to walk in love just as the Lord Jesus Christ loved us. Pray and ask the Lord to give you a submissive and humble heart. Pray that you will follow His example. Thank Him for everything—even the times when it is hard to follow His example. Thank Him for strengthening you with power through His Spirit in the inner man.

DAY TWO

☐ Read Ephesians

Ephesians 5:22

1. Read Ephesians 5:22-33. What is the world's philosophy regarding marriage? How is it different from the truth of God's Word?

2. Read Ephesians 5:22-24. What admonition is given to the wife? Whom ultimately is she obeying?

3. According to these same verses, to whom is the wife being compared? To whom is the husband being compared?

4. How do these comparisons help you understand the different roles of the husband and wife?

5. TRUTH SEARCH

   Compare Ephesians 5:22-24 with I Peter 3:1-6. Look for the things that please the Lord and record the benefits of being submissive.

6. Using Scripture to support your answer, what is a wife to do when she does not agree with her husband's decisions? To whom can she turn for wisdom and strength?

7. Considering the passage in I Peter 2:18-24, how can looking at and following the Lord's example help a wife to be submissive?

8. In everything we are called to do in Scripture we are ultimately submitting to the Lord Jesus Christ. Based upon all that you have learned in Ephesians, what should the primary motivation be for obedience?

Reflection

All over the world today there are countless philosophies regarding the role of a wife. But regardless of what the world thinks, God's Word stands as truth. Properly understood, the submissive spirit of a wife is a beautiful thing that reflects the humility and submission of our Lord Jesus Christ. If you are a wife, pray that you will be one who imitates God in every respect, especially in the marriage relationship. Pray for the men and women around you who are married. Pray that their relationships will bring glory and honor to the Lord.

DAY THREE

☐ Read Ephesians

Ephesians 5:23-33

1. Ephesians 5:21 tells us to be "subject to one another in the fear of Christ." Whom does this admonition apply to?

2. Why is it important that a man recognizes his call to be the "head of the wife" (Ephesians 5:23)?

3. a. Read Ephesians 5:25-31. What is the primary admonition given to the husband?

   b. Why would obeying the Lord by loving his wife help him in his attitude as the head of the home?

4. How does Ephesians 5:25-27 describe the Lord's love? What is the ultimate purpose for such love?

5. TRUTH SEARCH

   Compare the following passages with Ephesians 5:25-31 and record what you learn about the role and attitude of the husband: Colossians 3:19; I Peter 2:18-24; 3:7.

6. a. Define: "cleave"

   b. Why does marriage involve a man "leaving his father and mother and cleaving to his wife?"

   c. What are the results if he does not obey this command? What are the results if he does?

7. a. Why is marriage a picture of Christ and His relationship with the church (His body)?

   b. How can marriage be a witness to the unbelieving world?

8. What is the final admonition in Ephesians 5:33?

Reflection

Thank the Lord for the rich truth of His Word. Thank Him for giving us such clear instruction for daily living and daily relationships. Pray specifically for your marriage, for your pastor's marriage, for the marriages of the believers in your life. Pray that each would be a reflection and a witness of Jesus Christ to the unbelieving world.

DAY FOUR

☐ Read Ephesians

Ephesians 6:1-9

1. What is the world's view of families today? Give specific examples.

2. Read Ephesians 5:21-6:4. According to Ephesians 6:1, what attitude is a child to have toward his/her parents?

3. What commandment is given in Ephesians 6:2, and what is the resulting promise in Ephesians 6:3?

4. TRUTH SEARCH

   Look up the following verses and describe an obedient child: Proverbs 6:20-23; 23:22-25; Colossians 3:20.

5. If a child becomes a believer and his/her parents are not believers, does this change the principle in Ephesians 6:1-3? Why or why not? Use Scripture to support your answer.

6. a. Compare Ephesians 6:4 with Colossians 3:21. What is the primary commandment given to the father?

   b. What do you think this means?

7. Compare Ephesians 6:5-8 with Colossians 3:22-24. What words describe how a slave is to obey and what is to be his primary motivation for obedience?

8. What kind of attitude is the master to have toward his slave and for what reason? See Ephesians 6:9 for insight.

9. In what situations can we apply these principles?

Reflection

As you conclude your study today, pray through Ephesians 5:1-6:9. Pray that the Lord will give you the strength and power to obey His every word. Pray specifically for situations in your own life that require a submissive spirit. Thank the Lord for giving you the unchanging truth of His Word. Thank Him for showing you His will in relationships. Thank Him for giving you His Spirit to guide, direct, and convict you. Pray that you will be a man or a woman who follows in the footsteps of the Savior.

DAY FIVE

☐ Read Ephesians

Copy Ephesians 5:22-6:9 in the back of your book.

Walking with the Lord is a daily, minute by minute choice for each of us. Spiritual growth takes place as we spend time each day in the Word of God, and as we choose to obey His commands. Ephesians 4:1-6:9 is full of practical wisdom and clear instruction for the believer who desires to grow. Take inventory of your life before the Lord with this passage as the backdrop. Not all of these questions will apply to you. Choose one or two to focus on as you spend time before the Lord.

1. a. Look back to the prayer of Ephesians 1:17-23. In what ways are you growing in your knowledge of the Lord, or how have the eyes of your heart been enlightened over the past several weeks?

   b. What difference has learning about the "riches of the glory of His inheritance" made in your day-to-day life?

   c. How have you drawn on the surpassing power of the Lord to help you in your walk with Him?

2. a. Read Ephesians and note that the phrase "in Christ" is the most often repeated phrase of the book.

   b. Look carefully at chapters 1-3. How many times is this phrase repeated?

   c. Do the same for chapters 4-6. Why is this phrase repeated over and over again?

3. Consider all the references to the walk of the believer. What have you learned personally? Ask yourself the following questions:

   - What areas has the Lord spotlighted in my life that need changing?

   - Is there anything that is hindering me from walking consistently with the Lord? What must I do to free myself from this distraction?

4. Look closely at the prayer of Ephesians 3:16-21. How is the Lord strengthening you on the inside? Consider the following questions before answering:

- How has a greater understanding of the love of Christ made a difference in your daily walk?

- How could you make this more real in your life?

- How has knowing "He is able" helped you trust Him? What are you trusting the Lord for today?

Reflection

Thank the Lord for loving you, for sending His Son to die for you. Thank Him for promising you eternal life. Thank Him for giving you clear direction for daily living. Thank Him for the power of His Holy Spirit that enables you to experience victory over sin. Thank Him for His Word that teaches you about Him. Praise Him for letting us know Him!

"Finally, be strong in the Lord, and in the strength of His might. Put on the full armor of God, that you may be able to stand firm against the schemes of the devil."

Ephesians 6:10-11

LESSON ELEVEN

Stand Firm in His Strength

Ephesians 6:10-17

One beautiful Fall afternoon in 1993, I was in a taxicab on my way to a party. I commented on the lovely, sunny day to the driver. His reply was one I did not expect. He did not say a word about the weather, but instead told me that there was trouble going on in the center of the city. He was visibly shaken. I asked him what was happening, and he explained that there was some sort of demonstration going on, and that it was not good, whatever it was. I did not think too much about it, and went on to the party. Some of the people at the party had heard something was going on, but nothing definitive. We were all used to hearing crazy things because we lived in Moscow—the center of Russian politics. When it was time for me to leave and head home, I called Bob to let him know I would be walking home, and he insisted upon meeting me halfway. When we met each other on the street he proceeded to tell me that there was real trouble going on at the Russian White House (the Russian parliament building). We hurried home and turned on our television. We realized that the White House had been taken over and had been bombed! Within a few minutes of turning our television on, the news station went off the air—a very eerie thing to have happen.

> *I was running along the Moscow River and I saw in the distance, toward the center of the city, smoke from the bombs and fires hanging over the rooftops.*

Right at the time that this was going on, our church in Oregon was just beginning their morning services. We picked up our phone but only reached the answering machine. I began to leave a message, trying very hard to sound calm and collected. A friend picked up the phone when he heard it was me. I explained the situation to him, and he promised to let everyone know. Our conversation was recorded on the answering machine tape and was saved. I heard the tape some years later and I sounded like a nervous wreck! I guess I was! We went to bed, but did not sleep very well at all. We had no idea what might happen, but we were well aware of the danger. The next morning our good friends called us from their flat a few miles away. They were watching out their window as army tank after army tank rumbled down their street toward the Kremlin and Red Square. Later in the day, some other friends called us after hearing bombs going off in the distance. I remember attending a prayer meeting with other missionaries that day, praying not only for wisdom and safety, but also for the Lord's intervention. Amazingly, the Lord did intervene, and it was all over almost as soon as it started. The morning after it was over, I was running along the Moscow River and I saw in the distance, toward the center of the city, smoke from the bombs and fires hanging over the rooftops. Later that week we took a ride toward the White House. It was charred black, and much of the building had been severely damaged. The day went down in our "history books" as the "One Day War." I do not remember ever being so peaceful, and yet so afraid both at the same time.

As I recall the "One Day War," I think of the great battle that is going on in heaven—the great spiritual battle being waged "against the rulers, against the powers, against the world forces of this darkness, against the spiritual forces of wickedness in the heavenly places" (Ephesians 6:12). I am reminded that we have a wicked foe, Satan, the "prince of the power of the air," who is "prowling about like a roaring lion seeking someone to devour." He will go to any length to cause us to take our minds and hearts off of the Lord Jesus, to look at our circumstances and not at our Savior. The Evil One would love nothing more than for you and me to be half-hearted in our walk with the Lord; to be occupied with our fears, our wants, our desires; and to miss the richness and the blessing of following Christ. As we near the end of this great book of Scripture, we face the fact that we are in a battle—being waged in the heavens. Yet, it is a battle that so often looks like it is being fought right here and now. The apostle Paul, who knew more about troubles, distresses, fears, and struggles than I ever will, confronts us with the need to "be strong in the Lord and the strength of His might." The Christian life is not about us; it is about Him. It is about bringing glory and honor to the King of kings, and the Lord of lords. The victory has already been won at Calvary. We serve a risen Savior! May we learn to cling to Him.

As you begin your study of this section of Ephesians chapter six, ask the Lord to give you wisdom. Ask Him to help you understand what it means to "be strong in the Lord, and in the strength of His might." Ask Him to teach you how to be prepared to fight the battle. Ask Him to help you to bring glory to Him.

DAY ONE

☐ Read Ephesians

Revelation 2:1-5

1. a. Look at Acts 19:23-41. What kind of a city was Ephesus?

   b. Based upon your findings and the fact that you have studied almost all six chapters of this epistle, why do you think Paul began his exhortation with our wealth in Christ?

2. In order for us to have a healthy and enduring walk with the Lord, we need to be standing in, reminding ourselves of, and never ceasing to be amazed by the matchless grace of God. He has given us His Word to which we go daily to receive the spiritual nourishment we need to stand firm. Without spiritual nourishment and time spent at the feet of our Savior, we can so easily grow weary—doing the work of the ministry.

   a. For example, read Revelation 2:1-5. Which church is this passage referring to, and for what things was this church commended?

b. What does the Lord have against this church and why?

c. What does the Lord require of this church and what was the consequence for disobedience?

3. Why do you think the Lord deals so strongly with a church that has done all the right things?

4. As we begin our study of the spiritual battle, it is fitting to reconsider our love for the Lord, and even more importantly His love for us. John MacArthur writes, "As important as right doctrine and right living are, they are no substitute for love and, in fact, become cold and sterile apart from love. Lovelessness not only grieves the Lord but also gives Satan a foothold in a believer's life. When a believer, or a body of believers, loses its deep sense of love for the Lord, that believer or that church is on the brink of spiritual disaster."[1] What does it mean to have "left your first love?"

5. What danger is there in "walking the walk" without regularly enjoying the wealth?

6. a. Based upon your study of Ephesians and God's Word, what can you do to cultivate your love for the Lord? See also I John 4:7-19 for insight.

    b. How would you encourage a new believer to cultivate a love for the Lord?

Reflection

The church in Ephesus did not return to her first love and, as the Lord had warned, He removed her lampstand. "That church though orthodox, evangelical, and active in good works soon went out of existence."[2] How important it is that we, as individuals and corporately in the church, regularly remind ourselves of our rich salvation. How important it is to keep our foundation strong and secure, centered on Jesus Christ. The more we understand His love for us, the more we will love Him. Praise Him for His unending, unconditional love. Thank Him for making His love obvious at the cross of Jesus Christ. Pray that your love will not grow cold, but instead will grow strong.

DAY TWO

☐ Read Ephesians

Matthew 4:1-12

1. a. Read Matthew 4:1-11. To where is Jesus being led in this passage? How long was He there and what did He eat?

   b. What do you learn about the humanity of Jesus in Matthew 4:2?

2. a. Read Matthew 4:3-4. With what challenge does the devil present Jesus?

   b. What was the Lord's response?

3. a. Read Matthew 4:5-7. To where does the devil take Jesus, and what is the second challenge he presents to Jesus with? Keep your eyes on the text.

   b. What was the Lord's response?

4. a. Read Matthew 4:8-12. Where does the devil take Jesus next, and how does he tempt Jesus this time?

   b. How does Jesus respond and what happens next?

5. The temptation of Jesus is also recorded in Luke 4:1-13. Read this passage and record any additional insights you gain.

6. a. From a human standpoint, what condition was Jesus in when the devil began to tempt Him?

   b. How was Jesus prepared for these temptations?

7. What do you learn from Christ's example?

8. Consider our study of Ephesians 4:1-6:9. Why do you think this section of Scripture ends with a passage on the spiritual battle?

Reflection

The Lord Jesus was tempted by the devil when he was in the wilderness, after He had gone without food for forty days, and right at the time the Scripture says, "He then became hungry." Satan knows when we are weak and vulnerable. We must be imitators of Jesus Christ and stand firm in the truth of God. We must know the Word of God and our Savior better than anything else. Pray that you will be a child of God who is firmly rooted and grounded in the Word of God. Pray you will be "strong in the Lord and in the strength of His might."

DAY THREE

☐ Read Ephesians

Ephesians 6:10-13

1. According to Ephesians 6:10, what is the key to spiritual victory?

2. Read Ephesians 6:10-13 and write down everything you find that describes the battle.

3. a. Define scheme:

   b. Look up the following and record what more you learn about the schemer: John 8:44; I Peter 5:8; Revelation 12:9-10.

4. Describe a time in your Christian walk that you were accused or deceived. How did you respond? Why?

5. According to what you have learned in Ephesians, what must we do in order to stand firm against the schemes of the devil?

6. a. Why do you think it is important to remember that our struggle is not against flesh and blood, especially in light of Ephesians 4:1-6:9?

   b. Read II Corinthians 10:1-6. What more do you learn about the spiritual battle?

7. a. Define resist:

b. According to Ephesians 6:13, in addition to standing firm against the schemes of the devil, how will putting on the full armor of God help us to resist in the evil day?

c. In what ways do you find yourself having to resist in this evil day?

8. a. With Ephesians 6:10-13 as the backdrop, what have you learned about the strength of the Lord in the book of Ephesians?

b. How would you describe a "strong Christian" based upon your observations and study? Consider the prayers of chapters one and three. Think of everything that is yours in Christ. You may want to refer to II Corinthians 12:7-10 and Galatians 2:20 for further insight.

9. Ephesians 6:13 says, "Therefore, take up the full armor of God, that you may be able to resist in the evil day, and have done everything to stand firm." What is everything according to Ephesians 6:10-13?

Reflection

What are you doing to ensure that you are standing firm in the Lord? Are you prepared for the schemes of the devil? Have you put on the full armor of God? How important it is that we recognize our need to be 100% dependent upon the Lord, and 100% obedient to His Word. Remember our obedience flows from our understanding of our riches in Christ. He has blessed us with every spiritual blessing in the heavenly places in Christ. He loves us with an indescribable love. Surely it is in our best interest to fully obey His Word. Do not delay. Yield your life to Jesus Christ and let Him lead you to victory.

DAY FOUR

☐ Read Ephesians

Ephesians 6:14-17

1. As we consider the full armor of God described in Ephesians 6:14-17, what are we exhorted to do three times in verses 11, 13, 14? Based upon your study of Ephesians, how do we do this?

2. Look carefully at Ephesians 6:11 and 13. How much of the armor of God are we to put on? When are we told to take it off?

3. Read Ephesians 6:14-17 carefully and list each piece of armor.

4. a. From all that you have studied in Ephesians, what things are true of you because you are in Christ? Look specifically at Ephesians 1:3-14.

b. How does the truth of Christ help you stand firm against the schemes of the devil?

5. a. We have learned that we are righteous before God because of Jesus Christ—He is our righteousness. From all that you have studied in Ephesians, what are the results of our righteousness?

b. From what does the "breastplate of righteousness" protect you in the spiritual battle?

6. a. What is the believer who is "standing firm" wearing on his/her feet?

b. When we share the Gospel with unbelievers why is the gospel of peace our message? Use Scripture to support your answer.

7. a. What kind of "shield" is the believer to carry according to Ephesians 6:16?

    b. Faith is "taking God at His Word regardless of our feelings or circumstances." Describe a time in your life when you were tempted to depend upon your feelings or trust in your circumstances. What thoughts were going through your mind? What were your feelings telling you?

    c. How has using your shield of faith helped—or how would it help—to extinguish the "flaming missiles" in your life? Be specific—use examples from your own life.

8. The helmet of salvation is worn in the spiritual battle to remind us of the certainty of our future. There is absolutely nothing that can separate us from the Lord. Our eternity is safe and secure in Christ. Where in Ephesians can you turn to remind yourself of your eternal hope? Read Romans 5:3-5 and Hebrews 6:19 for further insight.

9. a. According to Ephesians 6:17b, what is the sword of the Spirit?

   b. Write out Hebrews 4:12. What does this verse tell you about your sword?

   c. Describe what happens when the soldier of Christ uses the sword effectively.

Reflection

Take some time and thank the Lord for giving you a full set of armor. Pray, asking the Lord to help you understand what it means to be strong in Him and the strength of His might. Thank Him for the truth that is in Christ Jesus. Thank Him for His righteousness that is now your righteousness. Thank Him for the peace that you enjoy because you have been declared righteous as a result of Jesus Christ's work. Thank Him that you have the freedom to tell others how they can find peace with God. Thank Him for the hope of your salvation and for His Word that is truer than your feelings and your circumstances.

DAY FIVE

☐ Read Ephesians

I Samuel 17:1-49

Copy Ephesians 6:10-17 in the back of your book.

One of my favorite passages in the Old Testament is found in I Samuel 17. What I love about this story is the way the strength of the Lord is displayed through the life of one very young boy. In many ways this story is a picture of the battles that we face every day, and the simple yet profound way God is willing to work if we simply ask in faith.

1. Begin by reading I Samuel 17:1-11. King Saul and the Israelites are facing the Philistines, long-time foes of Israel. As a heathen nation, they worshipped "Dagon" along with many other gods. As you will learn, the Philistines had no regard for the God of Israel or His children. What was it that "stood between them?"

2. Who was the champion of the Philistines? How is he described?

3. What words describe Saul and Israel's emotions when confronted with Goliath's challenge?

4. Who is introduced in I Samuel 17:12-19 and what does his father ask him to do?

5. According to I Samuel 17:20-25, what happened while David was talking with his brothers?

6. Continue reading I Samuel 17:26-30. How did David view Goliath's challenge?

7. a. Read I Samuel 17:31-40. Summarize what you learn about David in this section.

   b. Upon what past experience is David relying?

8. Look carefully at I Samuel 17:38-40. Compare Saul's armor with David's. What does this tell you about David?

9. a. How does Goliath view David in I Samuel 17:40-49?

   b. Goliath had taunted the armies of the living God for a long time. Discouragement and fear had set in, and they were not able to see beyond their circumstances. When David came with fresh faith, his brothers looked upon him with disdain, and Saul could only see his youthfulness. What set David apart?

   c. What is the end result?

10. a. What things in your life are large and looming like Goliath, and what is your emotional response to your giants?

b. Why is it important to remember that the battle is the Lord's?

c. How does David's example encourage you as you face your Goliath?

Reflection

We must stand firm in the Lord in order to fight the battles that He places before us. Pray that you will be like David, whose eyes were not on his circumstances. His ears ignored the discouragement of the people around him, and his heart was filled with faith in the living God! Pray that you will learn from each challenge to depend upon the Lord, and pray you will be prepared to face whatever giant the Lord places in your life. Fill your heart and your mind with the Word of God. Occupy yourself with the Savior!

1 MacArthur, pg. 333.
2 Ibid, pg. 334.

"With all prayer and petition pray at all times in the Spirit, and with this in view, be on the alert with all perseverance and petition for all the saints, and pray on my behalf, that utterance may be given to me in the opening of my mouth, to make known with boldness the mystery of the gospel, for which I am an ambassador in chains; that in proclaiming it I may speak boldly, as I ought to speak."

Ephesians 6:18–20

LESSON TWELVE

Pray, Pray, Pray
Ephesians 6:18-24

There was something very challenging about living in a place that was completely unfamiliar in almost every way. The living conditions were rustic and old fashioned; the public transportation system was used by the majority of citizens and was horribly crowded. The language was foreign to our ears and even the alphabet was different. At the time we lived in Russia, the government was very much in a state of flux. Because we were foreigners, we were always acutely aware of our surroundings, always trying to figure out what was going on, always trying to find a hint of familiarity and understanding in our new home. Because of the unfamiliarity, we would find ourselves fearful, never sure of ourselves or the people we encountered. We were very aware of the fact that we "stuck out like sore thumbs" because of the clothes we wore, the way we talked, the way we wore our hair. Even our wedding rings were worn on a different hand than those around us. As a result of being foreign, we had to be more careful with our money and our belongings for fear of being "ripped off." As I look back I remember how often I felt afraid and almost paralyzed by the unfamiliarity and newness. I also remember having to trust the Lord in ways I never had to at home—which was really so very refreshing (especially in retrospect).

I showed her the key and made a motion to the door, and shook my head "no" and then asked for butter (or maybe meat—the two words are very similar).

One evening, within the first month or so of our arrival, Bob and I returned home after a meeting on campus. We climbed the four flights of stairs to our flat and proceeded to unlock the door. For some reason it would not unlock! Bob stood and jiggled the key several times, took the key out, put it back in and jiggled some more. After a few moments I pushed him out of the way and proceeded to jiggle the key several times to no avail. Bob then started to get a little nervous, and jiggled the key some more. I went and sat on the dirty stairs in the dimly lit hallway and prayed. Then I got up and jiggled the key some more, gave up and let Bob try again. I sat down and we prayed again. Then I remembered that we had learned the word for butter in our language class. Maybe all we needed to do was dip our key in butter (because I did not know the word for oil) and it would open the jammed lock. So, as I would do in my own country, I went to my neighbor's door (whom I had never met) and explained in my very broken Russian that "I do not speak Russian," but I showed her the key and made a motion to the door, and shook my head "no" and then asked for butter (or maybe meat—the two words are very similar). She answered me with a cold Russian "no" and shut her door. Bob and I looked at each other and wondered what to do. So, I sat back down and prayed again, "Lord, You know that we live in Russia. You know that we do not know the language, we have no one to call, and we do not know what to do. Please, help us." We decided I should try another neighbor's door. No one answered. Bob continued to jiggle the key, and I tried it again just in case.

I will never forget that night. We felt so alone and so needy! We were absolutely dependent on the Lord. As I sat on the stairs praying, I heard a guy coming down the stairs. Bob and I had heard him before. He was, as usual, rather loud and drunk. He saw our predicament and proceeded to "help." He used all of the force he had in his shoulder to try and break down the door. Russian doors are most often about eight feet tall, and very thick. Needless to say, he only hurt his shoulder but did not budge the door. I tried to tell him that we needed oil, but probably succeeded in telling him "meat." He turned and left. I sat back down and we prayed again. "We do not know what to do, Lord. Thank You that You do." A few minutes later this same loud guy came back up the stairs. He was carrying with him half of a beer can. In the beer can was motor oil. He took the key from Bob's hand, dipped it in the oil, and proceeded to unlock our door. God had indeed provided exactly what we needed. A few minutes later there was a knock at our door, and upon opening it, we discovered Mr. Loud, bringing us a tiny container filled with oil "just in case."

The funny thing is that we faced more locked doors in our three years in Russia than we have ever faced in our entire life. The next year we lived in a different flat. Just days after moving in, our lock jammed. This time we did have a little Russian money in our pockets, we had learned where the pay phones were, and we knew enough language to call our landlord. He came within a few hours and chopped our door down with a hatchet! The Lord provides in all sorts of different ways.

The Lord always provides and is always present with us wherever we go. The challenge each of us faces is to make ourselves aware of His presence every minute of every day.

DAY ONE

☐ Read Ephesians

Ephesians 6:18-20

1. a. Read Ephesians 6:18-24. What is the final request Paul makes of his readers?

   b. How does he describe himself in Ephesians 6:19-20?

2. Why is an exhortation to prayer and petition a fitting end to this section on spiritual battle?

3. a. Look back to lessons three and five. What was the very first thing Paul requested of the Lord in Ephesians 1:16-19?

b. What did you learn about the Lord with regard to prayer in both chapters one and three? Use Scripture to support your answer.

4. a. Define prayer:

   b. Define petition:

   c. Define perseverance:

5. What attitude must we have in order to pray and petition? How is this consistent with what we have learned about the spiritual battle?

6. According to this passage, how often are we to pray and how is this possible?

7. TRUTH SEARCH

   a. Look up the following and record the words that describe our attitude in prayer: Romans 15:30; Philippians 4:6; Colossians 4:2, 12; I Thessalonians 5:17-18.

   b. Why is prayer a picture of dependence upon the Lord?

8. a. Paul asks prayer for whom and for what? See also Colossians 4:3-4.

   b. Why do you think the Scripture reminds us to pray for "all the saints" and for boldness in sharing the Gospel?

Reflection

It has been said that "prayer is hard work." This is certainly true in my life, and as I look back to the Gospels I find it to be true for the disciples as well. Just hours before the Lord Jesus was to be taken to the cross, He went to the Garden of Gethsemane to pray. He specifically asked His disciples to 'pray that you might not enter into temptation.' He withdrew from them about a stone's throw, and He knelt down and began to pray." He agonized in prayer before His Father, while His disciples were asleep! How hard it is to persevere in prayer, to petition, to be earnest in our prayers to the Lord. Yet, how important it is to recognize our need, and to take advantage of the privilege of intercession. The Lord inclines His ear to hear our prayers. May we be those who are regularly at His throne of grace.

DAY TWO

☐ Read Ephesians

Ephesians 6:21-22

1. a. Paul ministered to and with so many people. His heart for people is a real encouragement to us. What do you learn about his friend Tychicus in Ephesians 6:21-22? Find more information about him in Colossians 4:6-8.

   b. What do you learn about Paul's heart for the believers in Ephesus?

2. What kind of love does the Lord Jesus Christ have for you? Use Ephesians to support your answer.

3. a. Paul ends his letter with "Grace be with all those who love our Lord Jesus Christ with a love incorruptible."

b. Define incorruptible:

c. How would you describe an "incorruptible love" for the Lord Jesus Christ? Use Scripture to support your answer.

4. a. What have you learned about walking in love as you have studied Ephesians?

b. In what ways have you put this into practice in your day-to-day life?

5. Write out John 3:16. How has your study shed new light on this verse and others like it? Amazing love!

6. With whom can you share the love of Christ? Pray for boldness as you share the love of Christ with non-believers in your life.

Reflection

I have always found it challenging to realize that the New Testament teaches us to pray for each other's boldness in evangelism. The apostle Paul asked for prayer for opportunity and boldness in evangelism. Pray that the Lord will give you opportunity to tell others about your relationship with Jesus Christ. Pray that you will be bold when those opportunities come. Pray for other believers to be bold as well.

DAY THREE

☐ Read Ephesians

II Chronicles 20:1-30

The spiritual battle is fought and won when we are strong in the Lord and the strength of His might, and have put on the full armor of God. In addition, we must be communicating constantly with our Lord and Savior. It is of utmost importance that we are occupied with the Lord Jesus Christ, listening to His Word, and obeying His commands. In the book of II Chronicles, we are introduced to a man who found himself face to face with his enemy's armies. King Jehoshaphat sets a great example for us when we are in the heat of the battle.

1. Read II Chronicles 20:1-2. What was the report that King Jehoshaphat received?

2. a. Look carefully at II Chronicles 20:3-4. What was the King's emotional response after receiving this report?

   b. Describe a time in your life when you were faced with an overwhelming obstacle. What kinds of things went through your mind? What kinds of feelings did you have?

3. a. What did the King do in the face of the great multitude coming against him?

   b. What does this teach you about his relationship with God and in what ways does his example encourage you?

4. As you read King Jehoshaphat's prayer, record what you learn about the Lord, the king, and the people of Judah.

   a. II Chronicles 20:5-6:

   b. II Chronicles 20:7-9:

   c. II Chronicles 20:10-13:

5. a. When in your life have you felt fear, distress, or helplessness?

   b. Considering what you have observed in this prayer about the Lord, why is He the best One to turn to in the face of difficult times and spiritual battle?

6. According to II Chronicles 20:14-17, what are the King and the people of Judah to do as they face their enemies? Keep your eyes on the text!

7. a. Look closely at II Chronicles 20:18-19. What was King Jehoshaphat's response to God's instructions? How did the people of Judah then respond?

   b. What does their example teach you about facing your challenges?

8. a. Read II Chronicles 20:20-21. What is the King's battle plan?

b. Though the battle plan was unrealistic from a human standpoint, and based upon the character of God clearly outlined in earlier verses, why is this plan the best plan?

c. Why is thanksgiving one of the best weapons against the enemy?

9. What was the result of Judah's obedience according to II Chronicles 20:23-25?

10. a. Read II Chronicles 20:26-30. How did they celebrate God's victory?

b. Why is praise and worship a necessary element in our daily walk with the Lord, both individually and corporately?

Reflection

We have learned in our study of the book of Ephesians that the Christian life is impossible to live apart from the "surpassing greatness" of the Lord's power. We will face challenges and difficulties throughout our walks with the Lord, but we have been given everything we need to experience victory! King Jehoshaphat is a great example of a man who recognized his weakness and helplessness. When war was declared and fear filled his heart, he turned his attention to seek the Lord immediately! The Lord did not stop Judah's enemies from attacking, and His battle plan was not what most people would expect; however, He followed through with His promise and brought victory. King Jehoshaphat and his people obeyed the Lord and enjoyed the blessings. May the same be true for us! May we remember that the battle belongs to the Lord, and our strength and victory come from Him alone!

- What have you learned about the Lord from this chapter of Scripture that you did not know before?

- What can you take away from your study that will help you right now as you face seemingly insurmountable obstacles?

DAY FOUR

☐ Read Ephesians

1. Without looking at your Bible or your study, what was the main theme of Ephesians 1-3? Why?

2. Record what you remember about the following passages:
   Ephesians 1:1-14

   Ephesians 1:15-23

   Ephesians 2:1-10

   Ephesians 2:11-22

   Ephesians 3:1-13

   Ephesians 3:14-21

3. Who is the centerpiece of Ephesians 1-3? Why must He be?

4. Recall to your mind and then record all the things you can remember that are true of anyone who is in Christ.

5. What have you learned about the grace of God in your life?

6. In what ways have you grown in your knowledge of God?

7. In what ways have you been encouraged by the hope of His calling?

8. How have you experienced anew the surpassing greatness of His power?

9. What do you want to take from your study of Ephesians and apply to your life?

DAY FIVE

☐ Read Ephesians

Copy Ephesians 6:18-24 in the back of your book.

1. Without looking at your Bible or your study, what was the main theme of Ephesians 4-6?

2. Why did this theme follow the theme of chapters one through three?

3. Record what you remember about the following passages:
   Ephesians 4:1-16

   Ephesians 4:17-25

   Ephesians 5:1-14

   Ephesians 5:15-6:9

   Ephesians 6:10-24

4. Why is it important to walk with and serve the Lord as an overflow of our relationship with Him?

5. What have you learned about God's grace as you relate to others?

6. In what ways have you applied what you have learned from Ephesians 6:4-6?

7. What have you learned about walking in the Spirit that has helped you in your daily walk? In your daily relationships?

8. What have you learned about the spiritual battle that has been helpful?

9. Summarize what you have learned from the book of Ephesians in such a way that a new believer would understand.

10. Read Ephesians aloud. Thank the Lord for the rich truths of this epistle. Praise Him for saving you. Praise Him for giving you His Word. Ask Him to give you a heart to follow and obey Him all the days of your life.

BIBLIOGRAPHY

Campus Crusade for Christ. Your New Life In God's Love—Follow Up.
    San Bernadino: Campus Crusade, 1985.

Gilchrist, Scott. Ephesians Sermon Tapes.
    Portland: Southwest Bible Church, 1988.

Huffman Rockness, Miriam. A Passion for the Impossible.
    Wheaton: Harold Shaw Publishers, 1998.

Kaul, Grant. Notes on Hermeneutics.
    Portland: Southwest Bible Church, 1998.

MacArthur, John Jr. The MacArthur New Testament
    Commentary—Ephesians. Chicago: Moody Press, 1986.

Phillips, J.B. The New Testament in Modern English.
    New York: MacMillin Company, 1963.

NOTES

NOTES

NOTES

NOTES

NOTES

NOTES

NOTES

NOTES

AVAILABLE TITLES FROM CAS MONACO

Astonishing Love
A devotional Bible study on the book of First John with glimpses of the Gospel of John

This study of I John is designed to deepen your devotion to Jesus Christ, to draw you closer to Him as you spend time in His Word. In addition to enhancing your personal walk with the Lord and exposing you to His astonishing love, you will learn the mark of authentic Christianity and the key ingredient to genuine Christian living.

Living in the Riches Of His Grace
A devotional Bible study on the book of Ephesians

Explore the riches of God's grace as you dig into the book of Ephesians. Not only will you learn what it means to walk with Christ, you'll encounter the King!

Living Passionately for Christ
A devotional Bible study on the book of Philippians

This study is designed to ascertain the source of and the reason for passionate Christ-centered living. Discover what sets a believer apart, how such a believer will make an impact on the world—through relationships with family and friends, in the workplace, in sickness and through affliction. Stretch the limits off your faith for the glory of God.

Standing Firm in a World of Opportunity
A woman's devotional Bible study on the book of First Peter

This study, designed particularly for women, gives practical insight on how to stand firm in Christ in all sorts of circumstances. More importantly, I Peter highlights the Savior and the beauty of the gospel.

You can order these studies at Amazon.com

Made in the USA
Lexington, KY
14 May 2014